The Best
Stage Scenes
# of 2003

Smith and Kraus *Books for Actors*
YOUNG ACTOR SERIES

Great Scenes and Monologues for Children Volumes I and II

Forensics Series Volume I: Duo Practice and Competition: Thirty-five
8–10 Minute Original Comedic Plays

Forensics Series Volume II: Duo Practice and Competition: Thirty-five
8–10 Minute Original Dramatic Plays

Great Scenesin Dialect for Young Actors Volumes I and II

Great Scenes for Young Actors Volumes I and II

Short Scenes and Monologues for Middle School Actors

Multicultural Scenes for Young Actors

SCENE STUDY SERIES

The Best Stage Scenes of 2002

The Best Stage Scenes of 2001

The Best Stage Scenes of 2000

The Best Stage Scenes of 1999

The Best Stage Scenes of 1998

The Best Stage Scenes of 1997

The Best Stage Scenes of 1996

The Best Stage Scenes of 1995

The Best Stage Scenes of 1994

The Best Stage Scenes of 1993

The Best Stage Scenes of 1992

The Best Stage Scenes for Men from the 1980s

The Best Stage Scenes for Women from the 1980s

The Ultimate Scene Study Series Volume I: 101 Short Scenes for Groups

The Ultimate Scene Study Series Volume II: 102 Short Scenes for Two Actors

The Ultimate Scene Study Series Volume III: 103 Short Scenes for Three Actors

The Ultimate Scene Study Series Volume IV: 104 Short Scenes for Four Actors

Kiss and Tell—Restoration Comedy of Manners: Scenes, Monologues, and
Historical Context

A Brave and Violent Theatre Monologues, Scenes and Historical Context for
20th Century Irish Drama

Scenes from Classic Plays 468 BC to 1970 AD

If you require prepublication information about upcoming Smith and Kraus books, you may receive our semiannual catalogue, free of charge, by sending your name and address to *Smith and Kraus Catalogue, PO Box 127, Lyme, NH 03768. Or call us at (800) 895-4331; fax: (603) 643-6431.*

The Best
Stage Scenes
of 2003

edited by D. L. Lepidus

SCENE STUDY SERIES

A SMITH AND KRAUS BOOK

Published by Smith and Kraus, Inc.
177 Lyme Road, Hanover, NH 03755
www.SmithKraus.com

© 2004 by Smith and Kraus, Inc.
All rights reserved
Manufactured in the United States of America

First Edition: April 2004
10 9 8 7 6 5 4 3 2 1

Cover illustration by Lisa Goldfinger
Cover and text design by Julia Hill Gignoux

The Scene Study Series 1067-3253
ISBN 1-57525-335-6

NOTE: These scenes are intended to be used for audition and class study; permission is not required to use the material for those purposes. However, if there is a paid performance of any of the scenes included in this book, please refer to the permissions acknowledgment pages 196–199 to locate the source that can grant permission for public performance.

Contents

Scenes for One Man and One Woman

Scenes for Two Women

Scenes for Two Men

Foreword

In this book, you will find not only some of the best writing for the theater of late, but also a host of scene material *useful to you.*

If you bought this book, or if you are thinking of buying this book, you are most likely an actor, an acting student, or a teacher of acting looking for material for your students. If you are an actor, you're looking for a wide variety of scenes you can work on in class or use for auditions. You need scenes with a dramatic arc, a compelling action, and characters you might conceivably play. It is my fervent hope that I have found such scenes for you, after an exhaustive search through all the plays I saw or read in the last year which, believe me, is a *lot* of plays. If, however, you don't find the perfect scene for you in this book, do check out Smith and Kraus's other scene books.

As in the other scene and monologue books I have edited for Smith and Kraus, almost all of the scenes herein are from readily available, published plays. You will find publishers listed in the Rights and Permissions section in the back of this book, including their Web sites. You can get the entire text from the publisher, or from a theatrical bookstore, because you really should read the whole play when working on a scene. I know you will agree.

Some of the playwrights whose work I have included will be ones you have heard of — but many will be new to you. All represent the rich variety of contemporary writing for the theater.

As always, many thanks to the authors, agents, and publishers who allowed me to include their scenes in this book, as well as to Marisa Smith and Eric Kraus for entrusting me with this daunting project, and to Julia Gignoux and intern, Erin Meanley for their invaluable assistance in bringing it to fruition.

D.L. Lepidus

Scenes for
One Man and
One Woman

Barking Sharks
Israel Horovitz

Dramatic

Annie and Little Eddie: teens

> This enchanting play goes back and forth in time between the characters as adults and as they were as kids. Here, Little Eddie and Annie are sitting on a beach in Gloucester, Massachusetts, looking at shooting stars.

Annie and Little Eddie sit together at the water's edge, looking up at the stars.

ANNIE: Look! There's another one!

LITTLE EDDIE: Beautiful as shooting stars are, I can't help wondering if they're not just other little Earths like ours, covered with people like us, screaming, "We're *falling!*"

ANNIE: September's beautiful, but, it's sad . . . summer ending, school starting up, again. Did you know T.S. Eliot lived in Gloucester when he was little?

LITTLE EDDIE: I did, yuh, but, why'd you think of that?

ANNIE: I was thinking that it was obvious his family were summ'ah people, that he never went to Gloucester High.

LITTLE EDDIE: 'Cause *September* is the cruelest month.

ANNIE: Exactly!

LITTLE EDDIE: I always liked September. Tell you the truth: It always used'ta make me really happy to go back to school.

ANNIE: You didn't go to Catholic schools. You weren't taught by The Little Sisters of No Mercy!

LITTLE EDDIE: I do well in school. I'm not bragging I'm just saying that I *don't* do that well when I'm *away* from school. When I was growing up, I was totally miserable from Memorial Day til Labor Day. I'd have to say July is the cruelest month, and the 4th of July is definitely the most depressing major holiday.

ANNIE: What did you do, summers, mostly?

LITTLE EDDIE: Before now? Before this summer?

ANNIE: Yuh.

LITTLE EDDIE: We used'ta go to this island off the coast of France, every July, from the time I was five til, well, now.

ANNIE: Wow!

LITTLE EDDIE: We had this little old farmhouse. My father used to spend all his time reading books on philosophy, in French. My mother used'ta read about a thousand novels. My main job was to hang around and be quiet. I spent two Julys in a boys' sleep-over sports camp in, uh, America, but we don't talk about it. Otherwise, I was on this French island with my folks, every summer.

ANNIE: It sounds really amazing! How come you hated it?

LITTLE EDDIE: I didn't exactly hate it. A lot of it was pretty nice, but, I never really knew many other kids there, and the language thing was tough for the first ten years or so. We did a lot of nice biking . . . beautiful beaches, and dealing with my father's bouts of Existential Malaise.

ANNIE: What's that?

LITTLE EDDIE: He would worry about whether or not he really existed.

ANNIE: All the time?

LITTLE EDDIE: Every day, until supper-time, then, he'd eat oysters and worry about hepatitis. My father worries a lot.

ANNIE: My mother says your father was really smart, growing up. Number One in their class.

LITTLE EDDIE: He is.

ANNIE: You speak French?

LITTLE EDDIE: Well, sort of. Bad French. Comme un vache du Bronx.

ANNIE: Can you say something to me in French?

LITTLE EDDIE: I just did. You never took French?

ANNIE: Latin and Italian.

LITTLE EDDIE: If I say something in French, will you say something in Latin and Italian?

ANNIE: Sure.

LITTLE EDDIE: I know this James Joyce poem that's really nice, that my father made me learn in French.

ANNIE: OK.

LITTLE EDDIE: *Ne chante pas l'amour qui meurt/Ami, avec des chants si triste/Laisse la ta tristesse et chante/Qu'il suffit de l'amour qui passé.

(*Translation: Gentle lady, do not sing sad songs about the end of love; lay aside sadness and sing how love that passes is enough.)

ANNIE: It's beautiful.

LITTLE EDDIE: You could understand that?

ANNIE: Not the words, just the spirit. It's beautiful . . . It's so incredible to hear this other language coming out of you. It changes you so much!

LITTLE EDDIE: For better or worse?

ANNIE: 'Til death do us part.

(Annie winces at her own gaffe.)

LITTLE EDDIE: What?

ANNIE: Say more in French. Will you?

LITTLE EDDIE: Oui . . . Tu, tu es trop belle. Je t'aime trop. J'ai tres peur quand je regarde ton visage. Tu, tu est trop belle.

ANNIE: *(Answers in French.)* Toi, toi, aussi. Je t'aime trop, aussi. Tu, tu est trop beau.

LITTLE EDDIE: *(After an astonished pause.) Shit! Merde! You lied!*

ANNIE: *(Smiling wickedly.)* I did. I lied. I've been taking French all four years.

LITTLE EDDIE: That was a really shitty trick!

ANNIE: I know.

LITTLE EDDIE: May I kiss you?

ANNIE: Si tu parle francais.

LITTLE EDDIE: Je t'aime, Annie.

ANNIE: Je t'aime, aussi, Edouard.

(Little Eddie and Annie kiss a perfect first kiss . . . filled with expectation, affection, and concern.)

Chain Mail
Frederick Stroppel

Comic

Danielle and Nicky: both twenties

> Nicky is becoming increasingly, absurdly, paranoid and Danielle is
> trying to convince him that his fears he is being spied on are
> groundless.

NICKY: Don't you know what's going on? Don't you know what terrible
things are happening out there?

DANIELLE: In the hallway?

NICKY: In the world! The world is teeming with horrors! Nightmares!
Plagues real and metaphorical! People being killed, persecuted, en-
slaved — enduring sufferings and deprivations of body and soul on
a scale we can scarcely fathom. Why them? Why not *me?* Why should
I be spared? Because I'm *special?* No, I always knew this day was coming; it was only a matter of time. Sooner or later they had to find
me, zero in, trial and error, process of elimination . . . And now it's
here, right here! This letter with no return address, no distinguish-
ing features, nothing about it but an inescapable aura of doom —
why was it sent to *me,* and why today? Because it's *my turn!*

DANIELLE: Nicky — I can't listen anymore. You're not making any sense.

NICKY: Does it make sense to be beaten to death, or raped by your parents, or tortured and mutilated by the friendly cop on the corner?
No, but it's happening, isn't it, right in this city, right this very minute!
You could be walking down the street right now, whistling your happy
tune, enveloped in your cozy cocoon of ignorance, and then suddenly you're face down on the sidewalk, drowning in your own blood,
cut down by a bullet or a box-cutter or a runaway cab or an exploding
gas main . . . Anything! For no reason! Is there sense in that? Is that
logical?

DANIELLE: But you're talking as if it *were* logical, Nicky. You're talking as if it were part of some huge plot, all worked out and predestined, when in fact all those things you just mentioned are totally random, totally uncontrolled. Yes, bad things happen — good things happen, too. I know you've been depressed lately, and things haven't been breaking the way you wanted, but it's going to get better. I promise. Stop imagining the worst.

(Beat.)

NICKY: I never told you this, Danielle . . . About a month ago I was taking the subway home. And when I got off at Astor Place I was stopped by a man who said he was a detective. He showed me a photo of a little girl, said she was missing, wondered if I'd seen her. And I said no, I hadn't, which was true. Then he asked me my name and address. *My* name, *my* address. Why? I knew nothing about the case; why would he need to get in touch with me?

DANIELLE: *(Shrugs.)* Standard police procedure, I suppose.

NICKY: Standard police procedure, to keep tabs on people who have nothing to do with anything? I told him my name was Arthur Welk, and I lived all the way across town. West 24th Street. He probably knew I was lying, but I didn't care.

DANIELLE: *(Laughs.)* Arthur Welk? Where did you come up with that name?

NICKY: Then I come home, I turn on the news, and they're talking about the little girl. And it turns out she'd been found that morning, in a sewer drain, already dead. You remember that story.

DANIELLE: Oh, yes, that was terrible. Her poor parents . . .

NICKY: But that morning! You see? He's asking me where she is, and he already knows. What does that tell you?

DANIELLE: Maybe he was looking for the guy who did it.

NICKY: They *had* the guy who did it. The fucking piano teacher. They picked him up that afternoon. *Before* they talked to me, OK?

DANIELLE: Maybe this one detective hadn't been told.

NICKY: "Maybe, maybe" — you're getting some amazing fucking mileage out of that word. Of course he'd been told. He knew, he already knew. He wasn't looking for that little girl. It had nothing to do with that little girl. He was looking for me. *(Danielle is skeptical.)* All right, try this. Last week I got a phone call. Somebody's trying to sell me a credit card. Platinum Visa. Now you *know* my credit history.

DANIELLE: That doesn't matter. They call everybody.

NICKY: Of course they do. That's the beauty of this whole operation. It's all explainable. They're offering a great APR, like 4 percent — preapproved — consolidate your debts — blah blah blah . . . So I figure, what have I got to lose? Not thinking, you understand. So then they switch me to an independent verifier, some woman who has to check all the information, and the next thing I know I'm giving away my address. Not thinking. And then I realize, and I hang up, but it's too late. They have it. They know where I live.

DANIELLE: Nicky — they need your address if they're going to send you a credit card.

NICKY: They're *not* sending me a card. It was a trick, don't you understand? They wanted my address. My location. And here it is, written as plain as day on this fucking envelope. A 4 percent APR! What was I thinking?

DANIELLE: So you think this detective and the credit card company are somehow connected?

NICKY: It was the same voice.

DANIELLE: The same voice? The detective was a man, and this verifier was a woman . . .

NICKY: It was the same voice! Two different people, maybe but *the same voice! (Danielle stares at him.)* You just don't understand, do you?

DANIELLE: I want to, Nicky, but it has to make *some* kind of sense.

NICKY: It's not supposed to! They want it to sound crazy! They want me to be a voice crying in the wilderness! That's how they took care of all the others!

DANIELLE: What others?

NICKY: The others you never heard of! Because they took care of them! I'm about to disappear, Dani! I'm about to vanish! And when I'm gone, what will you say? "He started acting crazy near the end." Playing right into their hands! Just as they wanted, just as they planned!

DANIELLE: But who is "they"? Can you just tell me that?

NICKY: If I could tell you that . . . ! *(Frustrated.)* Ahh! What's the point in talking to you? For Christ's sake! You don't have a clue.

DANIELLE: *(Derisive.)* Oh, I have a clue.

    (Beat.)

NICKY: Do you?

DANIELLE: What?

NICKY: Do you have a clue?

DANIELLE: What are you getting at now?

NICKY: What are *you* getting at? Why are you so eager for me to open this letter? Why did you say "they" before? Do you know who sent it?

DANIELLE: No . . .

NICKY: Did you send it? Did you?

DANIELLE: Jesus, why did I bother to come home today?

NICKY: Is that it? What are you trying to do to me?

DANIELLE: You know, I wish you were on medication so I could tell you to double up.

NICKY: *(Grabs her arm.)* You think that's funny, Dani? You getting a kick out of all this?

DANIELLE: What are you grabbing me for?

NICKY: Tell me it's you. Tell me you're the one behind this. I'd almost be happy if I knew it were you.

DANIELLE: Let go!

NICKY: Or maybe the letter's *about* you. Is that it? Maybe someone is spreading lies about you. Trying to ruin our relationship. Trying to destroy my faith in you. Are they lies, Dani? Are they?

DANIELLE: You're hurting me!

NICKY: You think that hurts? *(Nicky slaps her hard across the face.)* How is that in comparison? Hurts a little more, doesn't it?

DANIELLE: *(Staggers back.)* What the fuck is wrong with you? You hit me!

NICKY: I know. And I've never hit you before, have I? You see — it's begun.

    (Danielle stares at him a moment.)

DANIELLE: I'm calling the police.

    (Danielle goes to the phone. Nicky is right behind her. He rips the phone cord from the wall.)

NICKY: You're not calling the police, you're calling *them*. It's all set up, isn't it? They're waiting right outside.

    (He goes to the window.)

DANIELLE: Nicky, listen to me — you need help. You're out of your mind.

NICKY: Of course I am. That's what you're supposed to believe.

DANIELLE: There's no one out there!

NICKY: Of course not. There's just you and me, in our little bit of paradise.

DANIELLE: I'm not taking this shit anymore. I'm leaving.

NICKY: So you can give them the signal? So you can say, "He's up there, waiting for you. Save me a bloody piece of his heart as a souvenir." *(Danielle heads for the door. Nicky rushes after her.)* You're not leaving!

DANIELLE: *(Wards him off.)* Nicky, please don't touch me. You're really scaring me, OK? I'm terrified, and I want to go.

(Nicky stares at her, then slowly backs off.)

NICKY: I suppose it wouldn't do any good. It's a timing thing, isn't it? If you don't come out in ten minutes anyway . . . All right. Go. *(Goes back to the table, sits.)* I've seen this coming all along. If I couldn't escape before, how can I escape now?

DANIELLE: Nicky — I'm going to bring some people back.

NICKY: Yes, I know.

DANIELLE: People who can *help* you.

NICKY: *(Smiles grimly.)* I understand.

DANIELLE: *(Comes back to the table.)* No, you don't understand! You don't know what's going on! Look! *(She picks up the letter, rips it into pieces.)* Look! See? No explosion, no poison darts, no sky falling. Nothing. Just a letter. A stupid fucking letter!

NICKY: I never knew when it would come, or how it would come. But one thing I knew, always: When the moment came, you would leave me. When the moment came, I would be alone.

DANIELLE: You *are* alone! And you brought it on yourself! You made this happen, you wished this insanity into being, and now you're stuck with it, because I've had enough! I'm sick of it! Why would anybody want to kill you? Why would anybody give a shit? *(She grabs her handbag and coat.)* And I'm not coming back this time. I told you, if you ever hit me . . . You crazy fucked-up idiot. There's chicken and rice in the kitchen. Make you own fucking dinner. *(As she heads for the door — there is a knock. Danielle is startled. Nicky nods, in grim acceptance. Whispering.)* Who's that?

NICKY: Who in-fucking-deed?

DANIELLE: Someone must have left the downstairs door open.

> *(Another knock, slow and chilling.)*

NICKY: So go answer it.

> *(Danielle hesitates.)*

DANIELLE: Why should I? We don't have to answer it.

NICKY: No, we don't. We can stay in here forever. We have Oreos up the ass.

> *(They wait in silence.)*

DANIELLE: This is crazy. I'm thinking like you. Why should I be afraid? *(Danielle opens the door. No one is there. On the floor is a shipping package. She picks it up.)* It's from L.L. Bean.

NICKY: Sure it is. Like what the fuck would I order form L.L. Bean?

DANIELLE: No, it's for me.

NICKY: Oh? What did you get? Seersucker shorts? Gore-tex mukaluks? *(Astutely.)* You didn't order *anything,* did you? *(Danielle is silent; she doesn't have to answer. Beat.)* Well, aren't you going to open it? *(Danielle looks at the package, afraid. Lights dim.)*

Chronicles
Don Nigro

Dramatic

Rhys (thirty-one); Alison (thirty-three)

> In the year 1901, Rhys has returned home to the Pendragon house, in the hills of east Ohio, after thirteen years. He's a respected journalist now, but he drinks too much, lives out of a suitcase, and has never been able to forget Alison, on whom he fathered a child, John Rose, just before he left home. He didn't know she was pregnant when he left. What he did know was that she'd just unexpectedly married his father, Gavin, an incredible act of betrayal toward him on both their parts, from his point of view. Before Rhys left, his friend Matt Armitage had revealed to him that Alison was in fact the daughter of Rhys' grandfather, John Pendragon. Gavin had married Alison to give the child a father and to prevent further incest, and he had lived with her in a chaste relationship until Gavin's death. Alison then married Matt Armitage and had three more children by him. It was only later that Rhys, who had kept in touch with the housekeeper, Sarah, learned that Alison had been pregnant with his child when she married his father. Now Rhys has returned home, unable to stay away from Alison any longer. Alison is happy with Matt, who has just been tactful enough to leave them alone to talk, but it is clear to both Rhys and Alison that they still love each other.

Rhys and Alison look at each other.

RHYS: I find it very impressive that he trusts me with you, under the circumstances.

ALISON: My husband is a very impressive man, in his own way. And he's been your friend all your life. He knows you. And he knows me.

RHYS: Apparently he does.

(Pause.)

ALISON: Rhys, I don't want to seem inhospitable, I really don't, but just what the hell do you think you're doing here?

RHYS: It's my house. I have as much right to be here as you do.

ALISON: I didn't say you don't have a right to be here. I just don't understand why you'd suddenly show up, completely unannounced, when you never even took the trouble to write to me, not once, in thirteen years.

RHYS: I wrote.

ALISON: You wrote to Sarah.

RHYS: Sarah's my friend.

ALISON: And what am I?

RHYS: I don't know what you are. Do you? *(Pause.)* I wanted to see my son.

ALISON: What son?

RHYS: My son.

ALISON: I don't know what you're talking about.

RHYS: Alison, I've had a lot of time to think this through. I didn't understand it when I left, but I do now.

ALISON: You don't understand anything.

RHYS: I know when John was born. I know when you married my father. And I know when you and I were together. My father married you to give you a husband, but Johnny is my son.

ALISON: He's my son, and as far as he's concerned, or anybody else is concerned, he's your half-brother, and that's the way it's going to stay. He's had a very rough time of it, Rhys. For most of his life he's been an incredibly moody, angry, unhappy boy. But he's better now. Matt's been a good influence on him. I'm not going to let you come back here and destroy that.

RHYS: I don't want to destroy anything.

ALISON: Then you can't tell him.

RHYS: I don't want to tell him, I just want to see him.

ALISON: And then you'll go?

RHYS: I guess it was too much to hope you'd be overjoyed to see me.

ALISON: Do you think there's been one minute since you left that I haven't thought about you, worried about you, worried about where you were and what you were doing? You're the one who went away from this house hating me.

RHYS: I never hated you.

ALISON: You hated me when I married your father.

RHYS: I didn't understand then. Why didn't you tell me you were going to have my child?

ALISON: Your father thought it was the best way.

RHYS: And you let him decide for you?

ALISON: What was I supposed to do? I was hardly more than a child myself. You were going off to college. I didn't want to ruin your life before it started.

RHYS: So you married my father instead?

ALISON: He never touched me. I never slept with him. That was part of our agreement. He would give the child a father. You would never know the truth. When he died, I didn't know what to do. Matt saved me. I owe him everything.

(Pause.)

RHYS: I guess it was nobody's fault.

ALISON: It was our fault. Yours and mine.

RHYS: Every minute you were thinking about me, I was thinking about you.

The Circus Animals' Desertion

Don Nigro

Comic

Becky (eighteen to twenty-two); Albert (fifties)

Becky Armitage, age eighteen, is in her slip. She is getting ready to go out to the carnival one October evening in 1945, in the upstairs room at her Aunt Moll's house where she lives with her two little girls, both the illegitimate children of a traveling carnival man Romeo DeFlores, who keeps impregnating her in the house of mirrors and then leaving town. But Becky is haunted by the ghost of her dead husband, Albert, the town librarian, who married her to give her children a father, but who went mad and hung himself in the barn when he realized she was still going to the carnival to meet Romeo. Becky is a pretty and charming but lost girl whose mother Jessie died when she was born. She doesn't mean to hurt anybody, but her nervous and rather scatterbrained approach to life gets her and the people who love her into trouble a lot. She's singing a forties' swing tune that she seems to be making up as she goes along, when Albert's ghost appears.

Sound of faint calliope music. Lights up on Becky's upstairs room at Aunt Moll's house in town. October, 1945. Evening. Becky in her slip, getting ready to go out.

BECKY: *(Singing absently to herself a forties' swing tune, not very recognizable.)* Boogie woogie. Boogie woogie. Boogie woogie. Boogie woogie. Doodliop do me on the jive, Clive. Doodliop do me on the woo woo. *(She is doing her lipstick in the mirror. Albert appears behind her. He is dead, rumpled, pale, and a bit greenish, but looks otherwise much as he did in life.)* Woo woo woo. Doodliop do me on the wooo woo. Doo doo.

ALBERT: It's a little crooked on the right side.

BECKY: Thanks, Albert. Doodliop do me on the — *(She sees him in the mirror.)* AHHHHHHHHHHH. *(She jumps, falling off her stool and smearing lipstick across her face.)* Will you stop doing that? I mean it, Albert. You've got to stop sneaking up on me like that.

ALBERT: I'm dead. It's my job.

BECKY: You're not dead. Well, OK, you're dead, but you're not here. Well, you're here, but not really. See what you did? I look like Old Weird Bertha who lives at the dump and has a pet rat.

(She begins wiping off lipstick and repairing her makeup.)

ALBERT: For there was never yet fair woman but she made mouths in a glass.

BECKY: Don't talk to me.

ALBERT: Sorry.

BECKY: You're not sorry. You like scaring me. Why am I even talking to you? I am not going to be crazy, Albert, do you understand? I am not going to be a crazy person. I'm going to be perfectly normal, or as near to that as I can fake, and I'm not going to waste my time talking to my dead husband any more. Christ, I used to make fun of you for talking to yourself all the time, and now I'm doing it, only what's worse is, I'm talking to myself and there's somebody here, and he's dead.

ALBERT: Where are the babies?

BECKY: They spent the day with Aunt Liz. They've been driving me berserk. Lorry screams and throws things all the time. She throws her food at me, she throws alphabet blocks at me, and when I change her diaper she throws shit at me. And June is all over the place now, and she's so weird. I mean, she's not exactly bad, she just — does bizarre things. She keeps trying to crawl out the window, and this is the second floor, and she hides in the closet and I have to go looking for her. The other day I had the window open and I walked in here and she had a bird on her head. A little bird, it was a wren or something, sitting right on top of her head, and June was just looking at it in the mirror and saying, "Birdy, birdy." Weird. And Uncle Clete is driving me crazy with his dumb jokes and his welding in the garage and slapping me on my butt in the kitchen, and if I hear "The Star Spangled Banner" played one more time on the tuba, I swear, I'm going down there and stuff that instrument up Billy's rectum. And I keep seeing my dead husband every place. Other than that, things are just peachy.

ALBERT: Where are you going, Becky?

BECKY: *(Putting on her dress.)* Out. I'm going out. I'm allowed to go out.

ALBERT: It's October.

BECKY: Yes, it's October, and the carnival is in town. So what? So what, Albert? You're dead. You're worm fodder. I can go anyplace I want, and you can't stop me, because you're rotting in a box six feet under out in the cemetery, so just go away and leave me alone, OK?

ALBERT: But you promised your Grandmother.

BECKY: I didn't promise her I'd never go to the carnival, I just promised I wouldn't sleep with Franklin Roosevelt, of which there's even less chance than there was before, because now he's just as dead as you are, only he's got the courtesy not to show up in my bedroom when I'm dressing and smear lipstick all over my face. And I also, as an extra added free bonus, am not sleeping with Harry Truman, either. So just stop looking at me like that. Why do you do this? Why do you come around here all the time?

ALBERT: I think you have unresolved feelings of guilt, so you're hallucinating.

BECKY: I'm not hallucinating and I don't feel guilty about anything, and I'm not crazy, and you're not here, and I'm going out now.

ALBERT: Don't go to the carnival, Becky.

BECKY: I'll go exactly where I please.

ALBERT: Stay here with me.

BECKY: I can't stay here with you because you're not even here. I'm going for a walk, OK?

ALBERT: Promise me you're not going to the carnival.

BECKY: I'm not going to the carnival.

ALBERT: You swear?

BECKY: I swear. I swear. I swear. Now, go and play with the other dead people, all right? Good-bye.

(She goes down the steps and out. Albert looks sadly after her.)

ALBERT: *(Looking in the mirror.)* Through a glass, darkly. *(Peering into the mirror.)* You're still in there.

The Circus Animals' Desertion

Don Nigro

Seriocomic

Becky (eighteen); Romeo (twenty-two)

> Romeo DeFlores is a traveling carnival guy who has fathered two children with Becky, but he has always then left town. Here, he comes back for her.

Night. The carnival in the park, Romeo DeFlores smokes a cigarette on the bench behind the Labyrinth of Mirrors. Carny music and the sound of distant thunder. Becky appears.

BECKY: Hello.

ROMEO: Hello.

BECKY: It's good to see you again.

ROMEO: Is it?

BECKY: Yes. You're looking well.

ROMEO: Am I?

BECKY: Yes. You always do. You look great. *(Pause.)* I missed you.

ROMEO: Did you?

BECKY: I did. I missed you a lot. I thought about you every day. Did you miss me? *(Pause.)* Did you?

ROMEO: How is your husband?

BECKY: He's all right. Well, actually, he's dead.

ROMEO: Your husband is dead?

BECKY: Yes. I'm a widow now. I'm an eighteen-year-old widow. The Widow Reedy. Old Widow Reedy. I feel old. I don't like feeling old. I don't look old, do I?

ROMEO: No.

BECKY: I've still got my figure. I don't want to be old yet. I still want things to happen to me.

ROMEO: What things?

BECKY: I don't know. Things.

ROMEO: Many things have happened to you already.

BECKY: Yes, but not good things. Except you. You're the only good thing. At night when I'm in bed alone I think about the times we spent in the Labyrinth of Mirrors, and it doesn't seem real, but that's partly why I like it, because it's so different from everything else in my life. There's nothing in the world like it. I missed you so much.

ROMEO: How are your children?

BECKY: They're fine.

ROMEO: Not dead?

BECKY: No. June is two and Lorry is fifteen months. June is quiet and thoughtful with these amazing eyes. She has your eyes. Very dark and mysterious. And she hides from me and birds fly in the window and land on her head. Lorry jabbers all the time and throws things. I don't know who the hell she's like. She's like a little monkey, except she's very pretty. I don't know which one drives me the crazier, Lorry because she's such a mess or June because she stares at me like Aunt Dor's cat. Like she knows something I don't. Gypsy eyes. Really scary. Why don't you say something?

ROMEO: What would you like me to say?

BECKY: Look, I know I wasn't very nice to you last year. I mean, not coming until the last minute and then running away and all, but I just — it was a really bad time and I was very confused, you know? And my husband was acting so weird and everything. But he's dead now, and I'm free, completely free. I can do whatever I want.

ROMEO: Can you?

BECKY: Why do you always do that?

ROMEO: Do what?

BECKY: Answer me with questions. It's like you don't believe anything I say. Like you're playing with me or something.

ROMEO: Do I ask you questions?

BECKY: There's another one. It always kind of puts me off balance.

ROMEO: Would you like me to stop asking questions?

BECKY: I'd like to ask you a question.

ROMEO: Yes?

BECKY: My grandmother said your family knew my family a long time ago in Maryland or someplace. She says the reason you people show up here every October is because you're always after the women in our family.

ROMEO: I'm waiting for the question.

BECKY: Is that true?

ROMEO: We come because we've always come.

BECKY: But she seems to think you're, kind of, out to get us.

ROMEO: Out to get you?

BECKY: Yes.

ROMEO: Do you believe that?

BECKY: I don't know.

ROMEO: If you believe I'm out to get you in some way, then why do you keep coming back?

BECKY: I don't know. I can't seem to help it. Pretty crazy, huh? So, are you out to get me, or what?
(Pause.)

ROMEO: How did your husband die? Did you kill him?

BECKY: No. He died of natural causes. He choked to death while hanging himself in the barn.

ROMEO: Why did he do that?

BECKY: He had mental problems. He was always kind of strange, but the longer we were married, the stranger he got. I guess it's the quiet ones you've got to watch out for, huh? *(Pause.)* Can I come with you?

ROMEO: Come with me where?

BECKY: I want to come with the carnival when you leave town.

ROMEO: Why would you want to do that?

BECKY: I really got to get out of here. I want to go places and do things. I've been trapped in this stupid town all my life. I can come with you, can't I? I'll work. I'll sell cherry drink and French fries. Or I can run the little floating duck stand. Maybe I could do some bareback riding. I communicate really good with horses. OK?

ROMEO: What about your children?

BECKY: They'll be all right. Aunt Liz will take care of them. She loves them. She'll be good to them. They love it on the farm.

ROMEO: Don't you want your children?

BECKY: It's not that I don't want them. I just — I want to put them somewhere for a while so I can have some adventures before I'm old, you
know? Can't I go with you?

ROMEO: But what if it's true that I'm out to get you?

BECKY: Then you've got me. You can have me. I'll surrender. Every night
in the Labyrinth of Mirrors. So what do you say, Romeo?
(Pause. Soft carny music.)

ROMEO: It's bad luck.

BECKY: What's bad luck?

ROMEO: It's bad luck to sleep with a suicide's wife.

BECKY: That's not bad luck.

ROMEO: Yes it is. To sleep with a suicide's wife means your children will
die.

BECKY: No it doesn't. Who told you that?

ROMEO: My grandmother.

BECKY: Well, what does SHE know?

ROMEO: More than you.

BECKY: Oh, please, please. I'm sorry I didn't stay with you last time, but
I'll make it up to you, I swear. Just let me come with you. If I don't
get out of here, I'm going to die. I mean it. I'll die. I'll turn into a
pillar of salt like Lot's wife. OK? Please? I'll do anything you want.
Anything. Please?
(Pause. He looks at her. Carny music in the background.)

ROMEO: Go home and pack your things.

BECKY: I don't need anything.

ROMEO: Yes you do. Winter is coming. It gets very cold on the road.

BECKY: Don't you go south in the winter?

ROMEO: It gets cold everywhere.

BECKY: OK. So I can come? I can really come?

ROMEO: I said, go home and pack your things.

BECKY: Oh, thank you. Thank you. I love you. *(She rushes toward him,
but he eludes her.)* What's the matter?

ROMEO: Not until we're out of town.

BECKY: I was just going to hug you.

ROMEO: It's very bad luck to touch the widow of a suicide.

BECKY: For how long? I mean, he's been dead since Christmas.

ROMEO: When we're out of town, the bad luck will be less. The further away we get from his grave, the better.

BECKY: All right. Fine. But you still love me, right? You do still love me, don't you?

ROMEO: It's bad luck to speak of these matters. Just go and pack your things. And hurry.

BECKY: OK.

(Becky looks at him, hesitates, then runs offstage. Romeo stands there. He throws down his cigarette and steps on it.)

DeFlores

Don Nigro

Comic

Holly (late teens); Bartolomeo (twenty)

> Opening scene. Holly Robey (seventeen) lives with her mother in a little house in Mary's Grove, Maryland, in the autumn of 1865. Bartolomeo DeFlores (twenty) has appeared at her house, asking for milk for his sick grandfather. Holly has supplied a bucket of milk, and she has come along with him to his family's camp in the woods to retrieve the bucket. She's come because she finds him very attractive, which alarms her a bit, because she is a good girl, and he has an exotic and rather dangerous but charming way about him. Bartolomeo and his eccentric family are traveling carnival people, not above the occasional con game, and his intention is to seduce her into running off with them.

> *The DeFlores camp, late afternoon of an early autumn day in the year 1965. We see the end of one of their wagons, with wooden door and trunk step, and various trunks and barrels. Holly enters, followed by Bartolomeo, who is carrying a bucket of milk.*

HOLLY: This is amazing. I've never seen anything like this. These wagons are so old. You actually live in these wagons?

BARTOLOMEO: *(Putting the heavy bucket down.)* We do indeed. All my life.

HOLLY: So, are you gypsies or something?

BARTOLOMEO: No, we're not gypsies, not strictly speaking, and take my advice, don't ever mention the gypsies around my grandfather. He gets very upset if you do.

HOLLY: Why is that?

BARTOLOMEO: Because we're not gypsies. Maybe we used to be gypsies. I think we were thrown out of the gypsies.

HOLLY: I didn't know you could be thrown out of the gypsies.

BARTOLOMEO: Oh, yes. The gypsies are a very proud people with a rich and complicated culture, but you must never mention them to my grandfather.

HOLLY: Don't worry. I don't even know your grandfather.

BARTOLOMEO: I'll introduce you.

HOLLY: Why did the gypsies throw you out?

BARTOLOMEO: Because we're not gypsies.

HOLLY: But how can you be thrown out of the gypsies if you're not gypsies in the first place?

BARTOLOMEO: Exactly. It's not fair, is it? Frankly, I wish we were gypsies. I have much respect for the gypsies. I think it was my grandfather who was thrown out. He seems to have committed some terrible sin against the gypsies. I don't know what. The story is different every time he tells it. In any case, we're not connected to anything, which means, of course, that we're connected to everything. You're extremely beautiful, you know.

(Bartolomeo takes her hand in both of his and looks into her eyes. Holly looks back at him, eyes wide, alarmed, for a moment, then pulls her hand away, backs into a trunk, sits down, stands up, and moves around to the other side of the trunk nervously.)

HOLLY: So, you're traveling people?

BARTOLOMEO: Yes. We're traveling people.

HOLLY: Where are you traveling to?

BARTOLOMEO: Nowhere.

HOLLY: You're going nowhere?

BARTOLOMEO: Yes, but we're going there very slowly, so we can enjoy the trip. When we like a place, or somebody in a place, we stay awhile.

HOLLY: But how do you live?

BARTOLOMEO: We're a small carnival of sorts. My grandmother tells fortunes when she's sober. My uncle Robespierre makes livestock disappear, mostly pigs, now and then a goat, when the goat is in a good mood. He has one pig in particular that he likes to make disappear, a very annoying pig, a spoiled pig, and also he's good at making food disappear. Now and then he has long arguments with the pig. You have the most perfectly formed arms, do you know that? I think the arms of young women are tremendously underrated as elements of their beauty, don't you?

HOLLY: Listen, if you could just pour the milk into something so I could have my bucket back, please, I've got to be getting back before my mother gets home.

BARTOLOMEO: First we must pay you for the milk.

HOLLY: Oh, that really isn't necessary. Just —

BARTOLOMEO: Please, don't insult us. We are a proud people, even though we aren't gypsies. We need milk for my grandfather, who craves it for some reason, and our cow died, may she rest in peace and romp in the fields of moo forever, and you were so kind as to give us some, and now we must repay you the only way we can — my grandmother must read your future.

HOLLY: No, that's OK, really. My mother is in town doing some things and if she gets back to our house and I'm not there —

BARTOLOMEO: Your mother has nothing at all to worry about. You're perfectly safe here, I swear on the Bible.

HOLLY: I don't see a Bible.

BARTOLOMEO: Yes, I think we lost it in a poker game. Well, then, I swear on our cow, Aphrodite.

HOLLY: I thought your cow was dead.

BARTOLOMEO: It's an old family tradition among persons who are not gypsies to swear on a dead cow. It's a very ancient custom. What is it? Don't you like it here?

HOLLY: No, I love your wagons. They look like old Spanish galleons, and it's so eerie down here in the woods by the creek, with the fog. Sometimes in the autumn we get these fogs that last for days. Very spooky. And you can hear the crows in the fog, and down here by the water the fog is so thick, it's like a dream.

BARTOLOMEO: I'm going to kiss you now.

HOLLY: I don't think so.

BARTOLOMEO: Yes, I think so.

HOLLY: No, I'm kind of busy this afternoon, so if you could just give me the bucket.

BARTOLOMEO: I will give you the bucket.

HOLLY: All I want is the bucket.

BARTOLOMEO: And believe me, you shall have it.

Doctor Faustus
Don Nigro

Dramatic

Faustus (forty); Mephistopheles (twenties)

> Faustus sold his soul to the devil, as you know. In this darkly comic
> play, the Devil, Mephistopheles, is a ravishing young woman.

*Faustus and Mephistopheles in bed, looking through a small window at
the stars.*

FAUSTUS: Bright circle of horned moon. When I behold the heavens, then
I repent, and curse thee, wicked Mephistopheles.

MEPHISTOPHELES: I wouldn't joke about such things if I were you.

FAUSTUS: Is God eavesdropping?

MEPHISTOPHELES: I am.

FAUSTUS: You're harmless enough, I think.

MEPHISTOPHELES: You're not.

FAUSTUS: Oh, but I'm a saintly man. Ask Wagner. I creep amid the plague
victims. I'm a kind of sanctified ghoul. Ask him.

MEPHISTOPHELES: He mentioned it.

FAUSTUS: He's a fool.

MEPHISTOPHELES: He is partly right. There is some tenderness in you yet,
as now, with me.

FAUSTUS: Those people are better off dead. Scrabbling about in squalor,
disintegrating with clap, the horrid, screaming mess of perpetual
childbirth. God. The doctor is cruel when he heals them. There is
no salvation in healing.

MEPHISTOPHELES: I think you are afraid of Wagner. He shows you what
you might be.

FAUSTUS: Be quiet and look at the stars.

MEPHISTOPHELES: I've seen the stars. You are not pleased by your virtues,
or by those who care for you.

FAUSTUS: Which is why I am so very much pleased by you. In hell is all manner of delight. Are you happier now, Devil? You seem to me even sadder. Have I not pleased you?

MEPHISTOPHELES: That is a meaningless question.

FAUSTUS: And have you not pleased me? Read my mind. Tell me.

MEPHISTOPHELES: I do not care to read your mind. I will never do so unless you force me to. But I can hear it working always. Your mind works so loudly, I must force myself not to listen. You are wondering now if I am a trap.

FAUSTUS: And if your flesh is quicklime, and if the Devil's tears are poison. Are they? Am I the dead man in the snow?

MEPHISTOPHELES: I would prefer not to discuss this, if you don't mind.

FAUSTUS: You do have emotions. You feel pain. You cry. You make love. You are tender with me. You love me.

MEPHISTOPHELES: This is a part of your damnation. You prefer not to see this, at present.

FAUSTUS: I don't believe that.

MEPHISTOPHELES: Yes you do.

FAUSTUS: I believe it may be a part of my damnation. I do not believe that you are without emotions.

MEPHISTOPHELES: You are a fool.

FAUSTUS: And a damned fool, at that. But can I be damned when the Devil loves me? Can she let me come to harm, and thus spoil her own great pleasure? I think not. I think the Devil is too selfish for that. Tell me that I'm mistaken.

MEPHISTOPHELES: The stars make patterns. You see them from one location and think you understand them. View them from another location and the patterns which seem real to you will vanish.

FAUSTUS: They don't vanish. They just form different patterns.

MEPHISTOPHELES: It amounts to the same thing.

FAUSTUS: No it doesn't.

MEPHISTOPHELES: I'm cold. We can make love again, if you'd like.

FAUSTUS: Is great Mephistopheles so passionate?

MEPHISTOPHELES: You are a dead man, Faustus.

FAUSTUS: You take a great deal of trouble over a dead man. I can only conclude that my case is far from closed. The Devil preserves me for reasons of her own, among them her misconceived and woebegotten passion for her victim. And, alas, his for her. It's true, Devil. Tell me I'm mistaken. You can't, can you? You know what I'm saying is true.

MEPHISTOPHELES: I trust you to be what you are, inevitably, to the inevitable consequences of what you are. You choose your own damnation.

FAUSTUS: And do you not love me, Devil?

MEPHISTOPHELES: You are lost.

FAUSTUS: One of us is.

The Fourth Wall
A.R. Gurney

Comic

Peggy (forties to fifties); Floyd (forties to fifties)

> Peggy has redecorated her living room as if it were a stage set. Amusingly, everyone who enters the room behaves as if they were in a play. Peggy's husband has asked a friend named Floyd, a local university professor of theater, to come over and maybe help Peggy escape from her delusion that "real life" is theater — and vice versa. Instead, Floyd begins seeing things Peggy's way.

Floyd entering.

FLOYD: Peggy! *(She stops.)* I have very bad news.

PEGGY: So do I.

FLOYD: You first.

PEGGY: I just received a threatening phone call.

FLOYD: Was it a man or a woman?

PEGGY: Hard to tell. It was either a man with a high voice or a woman who smokes at least a pack a day. Either way, it was suggested in very sinister tones that I rearrange my furniture immediately.

FLOYD: I can pretty well guess who it was.

PEGGY: Who?

FLOYD: Barbara Bush.

PEGGY: You mean, because of what I said about George . . .

FLOYD: They say she's very sensitive about her family.

PEGGY: But the voice was hoarse. Does she smoke?

FLOYD: I imagine secretly. I imagine she has to.

PEGGY: Well I'm sorry, these things should be said. Now your turn. What's your bad news?

FLOYD: I — I've decided not to tell you.

PEGGY: Hey! No fair!

FLOYD: I can't, Peggy, and here's why. You may have noticed that tonight we are caught in a death struggle between two sorts of plays.

PEGGY: Two sorts of plays?

FLOYD: One represents a uniquely American yearning for a truly democratic experience on a global scale. The other is a cheap throwback to a trivial continental sex comedy.

PEGGY: I don't understand . . .

FLOYD: I'm glad you don't. *(He looks off.)* But my job, as I see it, is to prevent the bad play from destroying the good. Which is why I won't sully this stage by telling you my news.

PEGGY: Does it have to do with my husband?

FLOYD: I'm not saying any more. As the watchman says in *Agamemnon,* "An ox stands on my tongue."

PEGGY: *(Starting offstage.)* Then I'll see for myself.

FLOYD: *(Quickly.)* No, don't . . . There's another reason why I don't want to tell you, Peggy.

PEGGY: Another reason?

FLOYD: I'm nervous that if you hear bad news, you'll blame the messenger. I'm not sure why, but I don't think I could stand that, Peggy.

PEGGY: I won't do it then. I promise.

FLOYD: OK, then. Here goes . . . You may remember I went off to tell Roger and Julia about the Saint Joan thing?

PEGGY: I remember very well.

FLOYD: I couldn't tell them.

PEGGY: Why not?

FLOYD: They were upstairs. In the bedroom. With the door locked.

PEGGY: What?

FLOYD: So I knocked. I even rattled the doorknob. Finally I put my ear to the door.

PEGGY: What did you hear?

FLOYD: Some of the most second-rate dialogue I have ever come across.

PEGGY: At least you heard dialogue.

FLOYD: Then they opened the door.

PEGGY: Were their clothes in disarray?

FLOYD: Somewhat. And they behaved sheepishly.

PEGGY: Sheepishly?

FLOYD: They claimed they'd been watching television.

PEGGY: That explains the sheepishness.

FLOYD: It also explains the lousy dialogue.

PEGGY: Did you tell them about Saint Joan?

FLOYD: I tried. But they shushed me. And waved me away.

PEGGY: Shushed you and waved you away?

FLOYD: And returned to the bed. Where they remained, sprawled on the bedspread, watching the tube.

PEGGY: No.

FLOYD: A sitcom, I might add.

PEGGY: No.

FLOYD: And a rerun at that.

PEGGY: Oh God.

FLOYD: Exactly. "Oh God." Actually, the line from *Saint Joan* is: "Oh God that madest this beautiful earth, when will it be ready to receive thy saints?"

PEGGY: Not if it's watching TV, I can tell you that.

FLOYD: Of course not.

PEGGY: I wonder what Saint Joan would do about this.

FLOYD: She'd ignore it. She'd have more on her mind than the backstage vagaries of a couple of stock characters.

PEGGY: But what if one of them is her husband?

FLOYD: Oh Peggy, don't let this throw a vulgar, domestic light on all we've accomplished so far.

PEGGY: *(Starting offstage.)* I'm sorry! They want sitcom, they'll get sitcom!

FLOYD: *(Holding her.)* Please, Peggy, stay just a little longer. I have one more thing to say.

PEGGY: But it's time for me to act!

FLOYD: Half of acting is listening, Peggy. I listened to your speeches. Now you listen to mine.

PEGGY: OK. But if I lose concentration, I'm sure you'll know why. *(She sits reluctantly.)*

FLOYD: *(Speaking with difficulty.)* Peggy, I want you to know that I have never, in all my years of teaching, made any kind of sexual advance toward any of my female students, no matter how attractive they may be.

PEGGY: Good for you, Floyd.

FLOYD: This is because I've always considered myself gay.

PEGGY: You're sweet to tell me. Now can I go?

FLOYD: No, listen. Please. This room has changed me. As we've played our scenes together, Peggy, I've begun to have second thoughts about my sexual orientation. Even as I've announced the infidelity of your husband, I've had the strange yearning to take his place at your side.

PEGGY: Floyd . . .

FLOYD: No, really. In fact, I think I love you, Peggy. I want to be with you wherever you go. All right, I may be gay, but why should that stop me? Gays on stage make spectacular lovers. English actors have been proving this for years. They may have the technique, but we have the feelings, Peggy. At least I have. For you. Tonight.

PEGGY: Aren't you slipping into the continental sex comedy, Floyd?

FLOYD: Maybe I am, but what the hell. Oh look, I don't have to sleep with you, though Lord knows I'd love to take a crack at it. I won't even play the frustrated lover, mooning at your side! May I simply hang out with you occasionally, screening your phone calls, opening your hate mail, maybe even sharing a pizza with you in lonely hotel rooms when you play Saint Joan on the road?

PEGGY: But what about your teaching career? Don't you want tenure?

FLOYD: *(Kneeling before her.)* How can I teach Saint Joan when I'm in love with the real thing?

Laestrygonians
Don Nigro

Dramatic

John Rose (late thirties); Jessie (twenty-four)

On a cold night early in 1927, by the railroad tracks just outside Armitage, a small town in east Ohio, John Rose, is trying desperately to help his immensely appealing but troubled sister Jessie. He's come home because he's very worried about her increasingly wild behavior. John has been a fine Shakespearean actor with an English touring company, been a soldier in World War I, and now is a leading man in silent movies in Hollywood. He drinks too much and sleeps with many women. His sister Jessie is beautiful, smart, funny, and overflowing with life and has always loved John with a fierce devotion that scares him, because in his heart he has always suspected that her love for him is much more than the love of a sister for a brother. She has written him long letters since she was a child, lived for the times when he's returned home, begged him to take her with him to Hollywood to be an actress. But he's spent his life running away from her, and from his feelings for her. Now her behavior has become so apparently self-destructive that he's been begged by their mother to come home and talk to her. Jessie has finally figured out that she and John are both the illegitimate children of their mother and their supposed uncle Rhys, and she knows that the only way she can be happy is to be with John. He knows it's wrong, and that it will kill them both, but he loves her desperately. In this scene, for the first time in their lives, they confront the reality of their situation, and their destiny.

John and Jessie, Armitage, early in 1927. A cold night. A railroad track by the woods.

JESSIE: *(Balancing on the rail.)* I knew you'd come. I just knew it.

JOHN: Didn't anybody ever teach you not to play on the railroad tracks?

JESSIE: I'm attracted to dangerous situations. I always have been. Once I went to Mad Anthony with some boys and we got drunk and I danced on the table in my underwear. And one time they dared me to dress up like a boy and go to the Crabtree whorehouse with them, and I did. I fooled everybody, too. I got all the way up to this poor girl's room. She never got suspicious until she put her hand between my legs. I was going to bring a sausage but I forgot in all the excitement. I told her I was the unfortunate victim of a farming accident, but then she found my breasts and threw me out. She was really indignant. She said, "What kind of a girl do you think I am?" The boys thought that was hysterical, but I felt bad for her.

JOHN: That isn't all you've been doing, Jessie. You've been climbing up on the old water tower in the middle of the night, breaking into abandoned buildings, driving down country roads at ninety miles an hour with that damned Jimmy Casey, speeding up to beat trains at crossings —

JESSIE: Don't blame Jimmy. It isn't his fault. He just can't resist me. Anyway, he won't let me behind the wheel any more since I drove his car off the pier and into the lake. I wanted to see if it would float.

JOHN: I'm not blaming him, I'm blaming you. Mother's worried sick about you. She thinks you're trying to kill yourself.

JESSIE: Not me. I'm going to live to be a hundred.

JOHN: Then what the hell do you think you're doing?

JESSIE: Getting Mother so worried she'd make you come home.

JOHN: You're telling me all this crazy behavior was some sort of stupid strategy designed to get me home?

JESSIE: I think it was a brilliant strategy, myself. It worked, didn't it? There you are, in the flesh. I rest my case.

JOHN: OK, I'm here. What do you want? I'm not taking you to Hollywood.

JESSIE: I can go to Hollywood any time I want to. Jimmy said he'd take me when his car dries out, or I could just buy a train ticket and go by myself. I've been saving up from my exciting popcorn job at the movie theater. I just don't want to go unless you really want me there.

JOHN: But I don't want you there.

JESSIE: Then what do you want?

JOHN: I want you to be safe and happy and stop acting crazy. What do you want?

JESSIE: You know what I want.

JOHN: I haven't got a clue, Jessie.

JESSIE: I've been giving this a lot of thought. Who is the one person you feel closer to than anybody in the whole world? Be honest now. Who?

JOHN: That would be you.

JESSIE: And who is the one person I feel closer to than anybody in the world?

JOHN: That would be Jimmy Casey, apparently.

JESSIE: No it wouldn't.

JOHN: Elmer the Greek?

JESSIE: That would be you, dumbbell.

JOHN: All right, that would be me. So?

JESSIE: I know what's wrong with us, Johnny. I've figured it out. I know why you've spent your life drinking and carousing with women you don't love and wasting your talent and running away, and why I act the way I do and why I'm never happy unless you're around. I know why. It's because we love each other.

JOHN: Of course we love each other. You're my sister.

JESSIE: That's not what I mean, and you know it.

JOHN: I don't know what you're talking about.

JESSIE: Yes you do. I've been in love with you since I was a little girl. I think you saw it in yourself the first time when I was fifteen, when you came home. Maybe it was just this glimmer of desire, this weird premonition, but it was there, just for a moment, and it scared you. And then when you came back after the war, when I was eighteen, that's when you knew you wanted me, and I wanted you, and it wasn't just some stray Freudian thought you'd had for a second. I kept thinking you hated me, but you didn't hate me, you were afraid of me, of what we felt, of what might happen.

JOHN: Jessie, this is not something we should be talking about.

JESSIE: This is exactly what we should be talking about. It's the only thing in our whole lives we haven't talked about, and it's the most important thing.

JOHN: You don't know what you're saying.

JESSIE: I know exactly what I'm saying. I've thought this all through, and neither one of us is ever going to have a moment's peace until we see what it would be like. It's the only way we can save each other. We have to be lovers.

JOHN: I'm not going to listen to this.

JESSIE: If you walk away from me again, I'm going to stand right here on these railroad tracks and watch the train come. You just try me, John Rose. There's a train due along here any minute now.

JOHN: We are not going to be lovers.

JESSIE: Jimmy Casey says it's a tradition in our family. He said Mother's parents and Rhys' grandparents were the same people, and that Rhys and Mother have always been lovers, and Rhys is really your father and my father, too.

JOHN: Why would Jimmy Casey want to tell you a thing like that?

JESSIE: Because one night I was teasing him about his parents being cousins and he got mad because I wouldn't sleep with him and told me. It explains why Mother and Uncle Rhys are always so weird around each other, it explains why Papa hated Rhys and hardly spoke two words to Mother since I was born. It explains why you and I are different, because the others are Papa's, and why we're her favorites, because she's always been in love with Rhys. It's our heritage, Johnny. It's what created us. It's why we feel so close. I could have married a dozen different men, but I've been waiting all my life for you.

JOHN: Jessie, it's wrong. Don't you see that? It's wrong.

JESSIE: Oh, great, Mr. Hollywood Casanova gets on his high horse and preaches to his sister about right and wrong. You've spent the last six years having orgies with half the women in California. You mean it's OK for you to waste your life drinking yourself to death because you can't stop thinking about me, but it's wrong for two people who love each other to be together even once? Why should we spend our whole lives avoiding what we both want because somebody decided someplace it was wrong? If somebody is being forced, it's wrong. If somebody is a child, it's wrong. I'm twenty-four years old, Johnny. I can make my own decisions. Nobody is being taken advantage of here. I love you. And you love me. Why keep making yourself as miserable as possible?

JOHN: You're the one who's making herself miserable.

JESSIE: I'm only miserable because you're being so stubborn.

JOHN: Jessie, I don't want you.

JESSIE: That's a lie.

JOHN: If that desire is in me somewhere, it comes from something evil in us, maybe it really is some curse from someplace back in the past, I don't know, but I know it isn't right. It's insane.

JESSIE: So you think we're both insane? Or just me? Is that what you think of me?

JOHN: Jessie, only bad things can come of it.

JESSIE: Bad things don't happen to me. I won't allow it. At night sometimes I get so lonesome for you I go up on the roof and walk around on the edge. It's like a whole other world up there. Mother keeps hearing things on the roof at night and she's convinced it's ghosts. Of course, I'm sure we do have ghosts. Sometimes I feel closer to the ghosts than to the live people, like I'm really one of them.

(Sound of a distant train whistle.)

JOHN: You're going to be one of them if you don't get off those tracks. There's a train coming.

JESSIE: Once when I read in a movie magazine that you were chasing three naked actresses at a party at Fatty Arbuckle's, I went out and walked down the middle of the road out by Witch Hollow, and the cars would go whizzing by. They swerved and swore a lot, but they never touched me. I really need to be touched. I go out in thunderstorms naked and dare the lightning to hit me, but it never does. I tease the boys really dreadfully, but I won't let anybody do it to me, not even Jimmy, because you're the only man in the world for me. If I can't have you, I don't want anybody else. I'd rather die. I'll take off my clothes and walk in the pond and drown. Now that Father's dead, there's nobody to keep draining it, so it's almost all back now. It's a sign.

(Sound of the train whistle, closer.)

JOHN: The train's coming.

(He reaches for her, but she eludes him.)

JESSIE: Sometimes I think I hear voices in the water, calling me. They'll find me floating naked in the water like they found that poor girl a hundred years ago.

JOHN: Jessie, the train is coming, now stop it.

(He lunges for her, but she gets away.)

JESSIE: It's either you or that, Johnny. There's no place in between.

(Sound of the train whistle, louder.)

JOHN: Jessie.

JESSIE: Just once, Johnny. Just once to get it out of our systems. Then we'll know what it is, and what it means.

JOHN: You don't really want that.

JESSIE: You want it, too. You can't tell me you don't.

JOHN: Jessie, it'll kill us. Do you understand? It will kill us.

JESSIE: Nothing's going to kill us. Why are you so afraid? I'm not afraid.
(Sound of the train whistle and the approaching train, much closer. John lunges for her and grabs her. The headlight of the train shines on them.)

JOHN: Will you get off there?

(They struggle on the tracks, and end up very close. They look at each other. She kisses him, a long kiss. He looks at her, still holding her. The train is very close.)

JESSIE: You love me. You do. You want me. You desire me.

JOHN: NO.

(He grabs her by the arms and throws her off the tracks, remains there himself, staring into the light of the oncoming train, but she runs back up onto the track and clutches onto him.)

JESSIE: You want me. You want me. You want me.

(Very loud train whistle. At the last moment he hurls himself off the track, Jessie in his arms, and they land upstage. John on top of her. Blackout, and the sound of the train going by in the darkness.)

Lobster Alice
Kira Obolensky

Comic

Alice Horowitz (twenties to thirties); John Finch (thirties)

> Alice Horowitz is a woman in her late twenties to thirties. John Finch, her boss, is in his early to late thirties. The scene takes place in animator John Finch's office, a few weeks after the arrival of the great Surrealist, Salvador Dali, who has unleashed both Alice's imagination and passion. In this scene, she attempts to recreate a failed date with Finch and to reimagine a past love affair.

FINCH: You're here.

ALICE: This is my job.

FINCH: I'm glad this is your job. Thank you. And I apologize for any thing I may have said or done that upset you.

ALICE: I accept your apology, John.

FINCH: Well, here we are Monday. Did you have a nice weekend?

ALICE: Oh very nice. Thank you.

FINCH: What did you do?

ALICE: I went to a party. To two parties. Fantastic parties. Filled with interesting people. Charming people.

FINCH: I don't want to hear another word.

(She's looking for something.)

ALICE: Uh huh.

FINCH: Have you lost something?

ALICE: Yes.

FINCH: What.

ALICE: It's round.

FINCH: Lots of things are round. Marbles. Balls.

ALICE: Not those. It's *fury.*

FINCH: Furry? With fur?

ALICE: Round and *fury.* I had it just a minute ago. And now I've misplaced it.

FINCH: It'll turn up. What is it? I mean, do you know what it is?

ALICE: It's a cottontail.

FINCH: A cottontail? What were you doing with a — Never mind.

ALICE: Oh well. It will turn up.

You want some coffee.

FINCH: Yes. I would like a cup. Wait. I can get it. And I can, uh, can I bring you a cup?

ALICE: I drink tea, Mr. Finch. Be right back.

(She exits.)

(From offstage:) Ouch!

FINCH: Alice, are you all right?

(Alice enters, pushing a white couch.)

ALICE: I stubbed my toe.

FINCH: What's this.

ALICE: It's my couch.

FINCH: Your couch. It seems familiar.

ALICE: It should.

FINCH: So this is *the couch.*

ALICE: This is *the couch.*

FINCH: Why is it here?

ALICE: Because I brought it to work.

FINCH: I'm sorry, Alice. I know I fell asleep on that couch —

ALICE: Yes you did. And when you did, it meant nothing to me. Nothing at all.

FINCH: Well, I was horrified by my actions. On that couch. I was like an animal.

ALICE: You were like a mouse.

FINCH: A mouse is an animal. And yet, you brought the couch to work. *(It occurs to him.)* Oh. I . . . should sit down.

ALICE: Please.

(Finch sits.)

FINCH: It's comfortable.

ALICE: I'm glad.

(Finch holds his arms open.)

FINCH: You are really something. This is really something.

ALICE: What is.

FINCH: That you went to all of this effort to recreate the scene of the crime. This is exactly what's been going through my head, day after day. Thinking, if only I could do it over. If only I could do it over. Sometimes I wonder if that's what life is. Missed chances that amplify in your brain, tormenting you like a drumbeat. If only I had kissed Alice on that fateful day. If only, if only.

ALICE: *I'm* not recreating the scene of the crime.

    (A beat.)

FINCH: Will you let *me* recreate the scene of the crime.

ALICE: Sure.

FINCH: *(Thinks.)* So. I had taken you out for a banana malt. At a diner you thought was boring. And you didn't like the banana malt. So, instead I take you out for . . . Cuban food. In West Hollywood, a little place with a banana tree in front. Oh, sorry. Bananas again.

ALICE: Yes, but different. More interesting.

FINCH: You know the place?

ALICE: I do.

FINCH: So we go there and we eat — what do we eat?

ALICE: Plantains, black beans and squid.

FINCH: My.

ALICE: According to the recipe books I've eaten. I've *read.*

FINCH: We eat. Maybe you have a drink.

ALICE: A Mojita.

FINCH: That's right.

ALICE: Rum and mint. Sugar and water.

FINCH: And then we get to your place. I ask to come in.

ALICE: I ask you to come in. For a beverage.

FINCH: That would be nice.

ALICE: You should say so avidly.

FINCH: That would be nice!

ALICE: As if there is no place you would rather be.

FINCH: That would be NICE!

ALICE: And you do not check your watch.

    (Finch checks his watch.)

FINCH: My watch is gone. What time is it?

(He looks at the clock on the wall. It has melted.)

Do you know what time it is?

ALICE: No.

FINCH: What are we going to do.

ALICE: You don't know? Remember, you're standing on my stoop.

FINCH: Oh yes. I wipe my feet.

ALICE: Why?

FINCH: For mud.

ALICE: I have never seen mud in West Hollywood.

FINCH: I suppose it's a reflex from the past.

ALICE: Shit on the past.

FINCH: What did you say.

ALICE: You heard me. The past is dead. The past is excrement.

FINCH: It's that man. He is not a good influence.

ALICE: He is a *fantastic* influence. I can't live in the past, anymore. I can't.
I have to break free. We all do —

FINCH: I don't want to argue with you, Alice.

ALICE: Good.

FINCH: I want to sit on the couch.

ALICE: Sit.

(He sits.)

I'll sit down here next to you.

FINCH: We discuss work —

ALICE: Only because you can't think of anything more interesting to talk
about.

(Finch thinks for a moment.)

FINCH: We could talk about our childhood.

(Alice sighs loudly.)

No really. It will be interesting.

ALICE: Go on. Tell me.

FINCH: I wanted to fly. An airplane.

ALICE: Don't most boys?

FINCH: Maybe.

ALICE: Well why did you want to.

FINCH: To see things from above. I always liked patterns. The Earth makes sense when it's so far away.

ALICE: Did you learn how to fly?

FINCH: Thankfully, no.

ALICE: Yes. Of course. Because things may have been quite different.

FINCH: Oh the war wasn't really an option. I have arthritis.

ALICE: You do?

FINCH: That's what the doctor said. Thankfully.

ALICE: I see.

FINCH: Lucky.

ALICE: Well. That's all?

FINCH: I guess so. *(A moment of awkward silence.)* What did you want when you were a girl.

ALICE: Dig a hole to China.

FINCH: Really.

ALICE: I started with a small spade and a beach bucket. I was very diligent.

FINCH: You still are. Diligent Alice.

ALICE: I only got as far as what looked like an open grave. And then my sister buried me alive. Now that was terrifying. I don't think she intended to, but I crawled into the hole. She put a handful of dirt in, I squeezed my eyes shut so the dirt wouldn't fall in. And soon I was completely covered.

FINCH: This is incredible.

ALICE: Only child's play.

FINCH: Did it scare you.

ALICE: To this day, I am terribly frightened of death.

FINCH: I imagine so.

(Awkward silence.)

ALICE: The small talk is over.

FINCH: Yes it is.

ALICE: And so I offer you an alcoholic beverage.

FINCH: I don't drink.

ALICE: *(Disapproving:)* You don't.

FINCH: My mother is a drunk.

ALICE: *(More interested:)* She is?

FINCH: Oh yes. Never touch the stuff myself.

ALICE: Makes sense. I spoke with her on the phone. She didn't seem drunk.

FINCH: Gin. It makes you tight. Did she sound tight?

ALICE: She did a little.

FINCH: I put my arm around your shoulder.

> *(He does.)*

ALICE: Nice. Very nice.

FINCH: Scootch in a little.

ALICE: *(Bolts up:)* Should I put a record on.

FINCH: You could.

ALICE: Jazz?

FINCH: Oh no. Please not jazz. It makes me jittery.

ALICE: *(Disbelief:)* It makes you jittery?

FINCH: All jangled up.

ALICE: It's supposed to.

FINCH: I never thought of it that way before. I could use some jangling. Let's hear jazz.

> *("You Tempt Me" on a scratchy LP from offstage. Alice sits again. Stands again.)*

ALICE: I forgot the beverage.

FINCH: No you didn't.

ALICE: That's right. You don't drink.

> *(She sits again.)*

FINCH: Are you nervous?

ALICE: A little.

FINCH: You don't need to be nervous.

ALICE: I'm expecting somebody else to show up.

FINCH: *You are?* What a cad.

ALICE: We don't know him yet.

FINCH: That's right.

ALICE: Still. Maybe he'll come. A boy I knew a while ago. Youthful passion. He was a soldier. He's dead now.

FINCH: And he's going to show up.

ALICE: He might. He really might.

FINCH: In the meantime, I'll just. There, arm is back in position.

ALICE: Snuggle in. You're warm.

FINCH: Am I perspiring? I hope I'm not perspiring on your shoulder?
ALICE: Shhhhh.

(A moment of silence. Alice closes her eyes and leans in. He gently kisses her on the hair.)

ALICE: Do that again.
FINCH: Like this?

(He kisses her again.)

ALICE: Again.
    Again.
    Again.
    (Getting faster.)
    Again. Again. Again. Again.
    Now.
    On my lips.

Masha No Home
Lloyd Suh

Dramatic

Masha (seventeen); Whitman (midtwenties)

> A half-built home. Masha, a seventeen-year-old Asian-American girl, stands in the center of the room with her arms raised high in the air. She's dressed in a school uniform and has been in this position for some time. Her brother Whitman, midtwenties, hovers. He's in a business suit, jacket off and sleeves rolled up, tie loosened.

Masha's arms hurt; she cheats them lower.

WHITMAN: Keep them up.

(Masha raises her arms higher.)

Higher.

(Higher.)

OK. Go on.

MASHA: So he's staring at me. I tell him to stop and he won't, I tell him again and still nothing. And so then I grabbed a pencil and I drove it through his thigh, just over the kneecap.

WHITMAN: Right, right.

MASHA: He starts screaming like a toddler, and I tell him so. And then the teachers are trying to pull me away from him, but not before I get a nice swipe across his face with my left. And then I reach for the scissors, 'cause he still won't shut up —

WHITMAN: Alright.

MASHA: But they were all over me by then; I dropped the scissors to the ground.

WHITMAN: Well that's good luck.

MASHA: I suppose.

WHITMAN: And this is when they called Annabell down.

MASHA: I suppose.

WHITMAN: Now this can't be. I'm on the clock downtown. A junior associate doesn't have the freedom to up and leave so he can pick up his ward from school — because I'm an *attorney,* Masha. I *work,* so that I can buy your food and your schoolbooks and the roof tiles over your head. You disrupt that, it upsets me. And Annabell, she's not fit to deal with these sorts of scenarios.

MASHA: Well that's her fault.

WHITMAN: Uh, no, see. It's not. If you hadn't stabbed this kid, she'd be baking a pie in the oven right now. She'd be fine, but instead she's confused and scared and nervous. She thinks you're the Devil, Masha.

MASHA: Not my fault she's a dizzy FOB.

WHITMAN: She's my *wife.* And therefore your sister-in-law; you will treat her with respect. She's my *wife.* Now. I understand acting out, I understand a little youthful rebellion. But this is another thing altogether. I may be your guardian, but I'm not the least bit interested in becoming your mother. What I don't want is a home out of control, and that's where you're leading us.

MASHA: My arms hurt.

WHITMAN: Yeah, and that's the point. If I'm to answer phones from distraught mothers and discontent school administrators, then you're gonna pay some penance.

MASHA: Right.

WHITMAN: We're gonna have some order here . . . I'm not a hard guy, Masha. If Mom was faced with this kind of acting out, if she could see your attitude lately, she'd be far harder than I.

MASHA: Oh I don't have to be reminded.

WHITMAN: And what does that mean?

MASHA: Means you're not Mom.

WHITMAN: I know I'm not.

MASHA: Good then.

WHITMAN: I'm not trying to be.

MASHA: I can see that.

WHITMAN: Good then.

MASHA: *(She drops her arms.)* Fuck this.

WHITMAN: Hey, arms up. Now.

MASHA: No.

WHITMAN: Masha.

MASHA: I'm not gonna indulge any Big Daddy fantasies you got here, *brother.*

WHITMAN: Just put your arms up.

MASHA: Not my mother.

WHITMAN: I said arms, up.

MASHA: *Not my mother.*

WHITMAN: But I'm your *guardian.*

(Silence. She puts her arms back up in the air.)

MASHA: Doesn't hurt anyway.

(Whitman chortles.)

Whitman. Doesn't hurt.

WHITMAN: So this should be very easy then.

MASHA: You might not be a hard guy, Whitman. Know what though? I'm a hard girl.

(No response.)

That's right. Arms in the air, what*ever.* 'Cause I'm too tough to get enough.

WHITMAN: Just wait.

MASHA: Oh I'm waiting.

WHITMAN: You know I spent a good deal of my childhood in that pose. That's straight from true Korean parentage, a slow torture; you'll feel it soon.

MASHA: *(Mocking.)* . . . *O-bbah! Nuh-mu nu-muh ah-puh . . . ! O-bbah . . . !* *(Oh, big brother . . . ! Oh, it hurts so bad, please big brother . . . !)*

WHITMAN: Shut it.

MASHA: *Aiya, O-bbah!*

(Big brother . . . !)

WHITMAN: I said quit with that nonsense.

MASHA: Oh but aren't I so helpless, Whitman?

WHITMAN: Arms, higher.

MASHA: And aren't you so big, such a big shot with the single-breasted suit and the swank Long Island home, dear little Korean wife and now a little sister daughter to take out all your shit on, oh Whitman you're like a daddy now ain'tcha, like a daddy you wanna be —

WHITMAN: Shut up. Arms higher.

MASHA: *(Suddenly; expressing a discomfort she's been pretending not to feel.)*

WHITMAN YOU MOTHER FAAAA OW JESUS IT HURTS AND
I HATE YOU HATE YOU HATE HATE HATE YOU —
(Whitman eases her arms down.)
AAAAAAaaaaaaaaaah . . .
(Whitman helps her to a chair, holds her arms in a resting position. He waits as she settles. Stands over her.)

WHITMAN: Alright then. We're gonna lay some rules down. Because seventeen years of age is too near adulthood for me to be your keeper; court sees fit for me to take responsibility over you, I can do that. But I won't tolerate infantile behavior, 'cause you're not an infant. And we're talking two months now, two months with Mother gone and you under my roof and this behavior is worse by the minute. Now *no more.* Understand? There will be no more pranks, no more barbs and fights and angry tirades at teachers and students. Or at me, or my wife. Got it? 'Cause my mother's dead too. If it's mourning you're doing, then we can mourn together. Not with fists in the school yard, not with outbursts and misbehavior, but here. At home, with your family.

MASHA: This ain't my home.

WHITMAN: Yeah well then what is?

MASHA: I don't have one. See? I'm an *orphan.*

WHITMAN: Lest you forget. So am I.

(Beat.)

MASHA: Scary halls and wooden boards around, can't walk to my room without seeing hollows and half-holds, like the roof is caving in; it's not a home.

WHITMAN: I know, Masha; we're building.

MASHA: I hate it.

WHITMAN: Look. You expect me to be someone. Don't know what it is, if it's brother or father or somewhere in between, but I made a promise to look after you. You act out and it *guts* me. Do you see? A call from your faculty, a fight at school, a failing grade, and another day of class skipped like it's nothing . . . Masha, those are *knives* in my *heart.*

MASHA: OK.

WHITMAN: Listen. Cries for attention I understand. Just tell me what you want.

MASHA: I want . . . *(Silence.)* I want a glass of water.

(He studies her. Frustration. Exits. While he's gone, Masha rubs her arms. Has a private moment of tears, sudden and full. She collects herself, dries her eyes before Whitman returns.)

Masha No Home
Lloyd Suh

Dramatic

Felix (twenties); Annabell (twenties)

> Felix, an Asian-American male in his twenties, stands haggard and
> run down in the doorway of a half-built home, speaking to Annabell,
> a Korean female in her late twenties. The house is empty, vacant.

FELIX: So he's not at home?

ANNABELL: Is it look like he is home?

FELIX: You know where he is?

ANNABELL: Why are you care so much?

FELIX: Are they together, Mash and Whitman?

ANNABELL: Maybe so, why are you care?

FELIX: Thought they were. You know. Estranged.

ANNABELL: You a strange.

FELIX: Ha. That's not what.

ANNABELL: Why you want talk Whitman?

FELIX: Got some issues to discuss. Between men . . . Got anything to drink?

ANNABELL: Milk.

FELIX: Swell.

ANNABELL: No drinky from boxy.

FELIX: Your English is marvelous.
　　(Takes a glass from cupboard, pours himself milk.)

ANNABELL: Fuck you.

FELIX: Now we're talking. Can I pour you a milk?

ANNABELL: No. I drink *soju.*
　　(Reveals a jug of rice wine.)

FELIX: Whoa. Can I get a pinch of that?

ANNABELL: One drink, you can have. Then you go.

FELIX: I'd rather wait for your husband.

ANNABELL: Then maybe best you drink slow.

(She pours, he dumps milk into sink and sits.)

FELIX: Deal.

ANNABELL: *(Raises glass for toast; he mirrors.) Goom-beh. [Cheers.]*

FELIX: *Gam-bai. [Cheers.]*

(They drink; Felix sips, but Annabell knocks it all back.)

FELIX: Whoa.

ANNABELL: You shut mouth.

(Pours another.)

FELIX: Everything alright at home, Missus?

ANNABELL: You tell me why you want speak to Whitman.

FELIX: Have some matters to discuss.

ANNABELL: Shut up and drink.

(He does.)

Why you not tell me what you are telling Whitman?

FELIX: I told you. It's between men.

ANNABELL: *Eh, sek-ee-nohm yah. [Ugh, fuckin' shithead.]*

FELIX: What?

ANNABELL: Shut up and drink.

FELIX: Are you drunk?

ANNABELL: My mother tell me is good to come America. Tell me I stop to work in mud and shit, maybe then I have some calm life. Some happy life. Understand?

FELIX: Sure, Missus.

ANNABELL: But secret of life and secret of world is: Everywhere you go, mud and shit. Understand? Come to America, learn is all shit and sucking. Nowhere in world is happy world. Come to America, think is any different? Bullshit fuckee! No different nothing; still same shit and shit fuckee.

FELIX: Ah. Yes.

ANNABELL: Now you tell me why you want talk Whitman.

FELIX: It's just, um.

ANNABELL: Eck. You fucking *man.*

FELIX: Uh.

ANNABELL: *Goom-beh!*

FELIX: Alright, *gam-bai!*

ANNABELL: You Chinese?

FELIX: Yeah.

ANNABELL: I been China. Fucking China, bullshit fuckee.

FELIX: That's lovely.

ANNABELL: Who you are?

FELIX: How's that?

ANNABELL: Friend of Masha you say, but I never see you before. What your name is?

FELIX: Felix.

ANNABELL: Feerick?

FELIX: Feee-Licks.

ANNABELL: What kind name is?

FELIX: It's my name.

ANNABELL: Stupid name.

FELIX: Hey.

ANNABELL: *Shee-gulluh! [Shut up!]*

FELIX: OK, you're mean.

ANNABELL: OK you are stupid man and I am tire of you not tell me what you want tell Whitman. Why you not talk me?

FELIX: Hey look.

ANNABELL: Because I not a man . . . ? *[Fuck you.]*

FELIX: . . . *Gam-pai!*

(Raises his glass, tries to excite with the flourish, but her gaze is fixed.)

ANNABELL: No! You tell me.

FELIX: I said *Gam-pai . . . !*

(Again with the glass.)

ANNABELL: Maybe I talk funny to you, but I no stupid. OK?

FELIX: OK.

ANNABELL: You talk funny to me, too. So now you tell me.

FELIX: I just, uh. I need to know what . . . you know. What kind of guy he is.

ANNABELL: *Muh-sun-mal-ee-yah? [What are you talking about?]*

FELIX: See, I don't understand what you're saying. When you do that.

ANNABELL: I don't understanding what you say too. I ask why you want do that?

FELIX: I have my reasons.

ANNABELL: I say tell me or I gonna screaming . . . *Tell me!*

FELIX: No, Jesus . . .

ANNABELL: Why you no tell me . . . ?

FELIX: Don't want to . . . ! Can't . . . !

ANNABELL: *Why You Wanna See Whitman . . . ?!?!*

FELIX: *Because I have his money.*

    (Stillness.)

ANNABELL: Who you are . . . ?

FELIX: I'm Felix.

The Nina Variations
Steven Dietz

Dramatic

Nina (twenties); Treplev (twenties)

> This play is a fascinating series of riffs on the relationship between
> Nina and Konstantin in Chekhov's *The Sea Gull*. Nina, of course,
> ran off with Trigorin; but she has come home, much chastened.

> *Treplev rushes on, embraces Nina, passionately. Nina remains seated at
> the desk.*

TREPLEV: Nina! Nina — it's you . . . it's you . . . all day long I've thought
this would happen! Just like my mother, I had a premonition — a
premonition that you would come to me!

NINA: I never left, Kostya.

TREPLEV: How I've *waited,* Nina! How I've waited for you to return! I
came looking for you every day! I called out your name! I kissed the
ground you walked on!

NINA: I've been here all along. Sitting right here, at your desk.

TREPLEV: I've been in such agony. Cold as a man in a dungeon. Alone
with my words — my colorless, melancholy words. I cursed you! I
hated you! I tore up your letters and your photographs — but now
— Nina, my darling — you've come to me!

NINA: Don't cry, you mustn't cry.

TREPLEV: Are we alone?

NINA: We're alone.

TREPLEV: Lock the door, so no one will come in.

NINA: No one will —

TREPLEV: Mother is here, I know it! Lock the door. *(He closes his eyes. She
does not move.)*

NINA: There. It's locked. Is that better?

TREPLEV: *(Eyes still closed.)* Put a chair against it.

NINA: Kostya —

TREPLEV: Please! *(She does not move.)*

NINA: How's that? *(Treplev slowly opens his eyes.)*

TREPLEV: Much better. *(He turns and looks at her.)*

NINA: May I kiss you?

TREPLEV: Oh, my love . . . *(He approaches her, hopefully.)*

NINA: I want to light three candles and kiss you. *(He stops.)*

TREPLEV: Why three candles? *(She removes three small candles from her bag [or the desk] during the following.)*

NINA: It is my wish.

TREPLEV: Yes, but —

NINA: Do you not wish to kiss me?

TREPLEV: Certainly. I wish it, Nina, I wish it day and night — but I was asking about the —

NINA: When I kissed Trigorin — in that stolen interval when my life seemed whole and possible — there were no candles lit. We kissed in wet, dark air. And from that kiss, our life to this moment ensued. So, now, Kostya . . . I want to kiss near a flame. *(She begins to light the candles.)*

TREPLEV: My mother is very superstitious. She has an unfounded fear of many things.

NINA: I am almost ready, Kostya —

TREPLEV: The number thirteen is one. It terrifies her — silly old woman!

NINA: There. Now, I will dim the lights. *(She closes her eyes and reaches an arm into the air, as — the lights fade out — leaving the candles prominent.)*

TREPLEV: And she has one other fear — her *greatest* fear, actually: *(Nina approaches him.)* That of three lit candles.

NINA: Yes. One for me. One for you. And one for mystery. *(She prepares to kiss him. He is fearful, motionless.)*

TREPLEV: Mother warned me — all my life . . .

NINA: Yes?

TREPLEV: "Three lit candles," she always says . . .

NINA: Yes?

TREPLEV: "Bring emptiness and despair." *(She kisses him, gently, seductively, on the mouth. She whispers . . .)*

NINA: And so, Kostya, who do you wish to believe? Your heart? *(She kisses him again.)* Or your mother? *(He stares at her. Then, he kisses her with great passion. She responds in kind. After a few moments, Nina pulls back and looks at his face.)* It's so warm here. So warm and so good. *(She blows out one of the candles.)* Do I look different to you now?

TREPLEV: Yes.

NINA: I was afraid you would hate me. Every night I have the same dream: You look right at my face and you don't recognize me. *(She blows out a second candle.)* And now, Kostya? Do I look different to you now?

TREPLEV: Yes.

NINA: Tell me that's only a dream. Tell me it's not true. Tell me you see me — that you see me *right now* — and that you know who I am.

TREPLEV: I *see you*, Nina. I swear it. *(She blows out the third candle. The stage sits in darkness.)*

NINA: And now? Do you see me now?

TREPLEV: Yes. *(Silence. Words from the darkness.)*

NINA: Never forget me, Kostya. No matter how black the night, no matter how deep the years — remember that I have written my name on you. I am the last face you will see before your death.

Oedi
Rich Orloff

Comic

Oedipus, King of Thebes (early thirties); Jocasta, Oedipus' wife, old enough to be his mother.

> Ancient Greece, around 4 P.M. In this parody of Oedipus Rex, Oedipus is working up the courage to tell his wife Jocasta that he has just learned that she is also his mother. Jocasta enters, just after Oedipus' advisors have left.

JOCASTA: I didn't know you were in a meeting.

OEDIPUS: It was the most important meeting of my life.

JOCASTA: More important than when we met and you became my blintz of bliss?

OEDIPUS: Jocasta, I must tell you something most horrible, worse than the most terrible news you could imagine.

JOCASTA: You didn't like my brisket last night?

OEDIPUS: That's not it.

JOCASTA: What a relief. I was afraid I used too many bay leaves.

OEDIPUS: Oh, I cannot bear to tell you.

JOCASTA: My toga's too short, isn't it? You think a woman of my age —

OEDIPUS: Your toga's fine.

JOCASTA: Are we having problems I'm unaware of in the horizontal department?

OEDIPUS: No, everything's fine in the — Jocasta, I just received the preliminary report of the Creon Commission.

JOCASTA: Oh, good. As soon as we name the murderer of Laios and make him drink some seltzer with a shpritz of hemlock, I know your approval rating will bounce right back.

OEDIPUS: I don't think so.

JOCASTA: Why not?

OEDIPUS: Jocasta, my beloved . . .

JOCASTA: Oedipus, my Corinthian column of love . . .

OEDIPUS: Jocasta . . . The murderer of your late husband stands before you.

JOCASTA: You killed Laios?

OEDIPUS: Yes.

JOCASTA: Oh, no! Horrors of horrors! I suddenly feel like plucking —

OEDIPUS: Don't pluck your eyes out!

JOCASTA: No, I feel like plucking a chicken. I'm so stressed. How are we going to put a spin on this so the public doesn't hate you?

OEDIPUS: Don't *you* hate me?

JOCASTA: Nah.

OEDIPUS: But I murdered your first husband!

JOCASTA: How can I hate you for something I thought of doing every single day of our marriage?

OEDIPUS: I thought you loved him.

JOCASTA: Feh.

OEDIPUS: You didn't love him?

JOCASTA: What's to love? The man snored, he had bad breath, and when I think of the things that man made me do . . .

OEDIPUS: You mean, in the bedroom?

JOCASTA: Worse, in the kitchen. I'd make him a nice roast chicken, and he'd make me melt some feta cheese on it. The man had no class.

OEDIPUS: But when I first met you, you were in deep mourning.

JOCASTA: My press people insisted. I wanted to go sunbathing on Crete.

OEDIPUS: I didn't know.

JOCASTA: So you see, my darling, the news is not that bad at all.

OEDIPUS: But I have not told you all of it, and the news that remains is so horrendous my lips can barely form the shapes to say the misbegotten words.

JOCASTA: Can it wait? In fifteen minutes, I have my belly dancercize class.

OEDIPUS: Jocasta, do you remember the prophecy of Tiresias that your husband would be murdered by your son?

JOCASTA: Yes. I also remember he prophesied *The Iliad* would never make it as a novel.

OEDIPUS: Jocasta, I . . . I cannot tell you. The shame is too deep.

JOCASTA: Don't feel ashamed, my beloved.

OEDIPUS: Please say no more. Your words of affection only make it more difficult.

JOCASTA: Why?

OEDIPUS: Because . . . Because there's reason to believe that, by some ferocious folly of the fates, you married your own son.

JOCASTA: So?

OEDIPUS: Did you not hear me? I'm your son!

JOCASTA: So tell me something I don't know.

OEDIPUS: You know I'm your son?

JOCASTA: From the first moment you came into town. I took one look at those eyes, that smile, that — oh, wait a second, you have a little shmutz on your forehead.

(Jocasta licks her fingers and begins to wipe Oedi's forehead.)

OEDIPUS: Stop that! How could you know I was your son and not tell me?

JOCASTA: I didn't think it was significant.

OEDIPUS: You married me!

JOCASTA: You asked.

OEDIPUS: I know, but —

JOCASTA: I would've been happy just dating; but you said, "Marry me, Jocasta, and I'll be the happiest man on earth." What mother could refuse such an offer?

OEDIPUS: But I killed Dad!

JOCASTA: So? He never liked you anyway.

OEDIPUS: He didn't?

JOCASTA: Once he heard Tiresias' prediction that you were destined to murder him, he insisted you be sent away. I said, "Can't we wait and see? Maybe he'll just wound you a little."

OEDIPUS: This is the most devastating day of my life.

JOCASTA: Look, you're here and all is well, so unless there's some more news, I want to get to my belly dancercize class. Next week we start navel exercises, so I need to be in shipshape.

OEDIPUS: Don't you think we have some issues to discuss?

JOCASTA: Like what?

OEDIPUS: Like the fact that we can no longer live as husband and wife.

JOCASTA: Why not?

OEDIPUS: Because you're my mother!

JOCASTA: You say that like it's a negative.

OEDIPUS: Men cannot marry their mothers!

JOCASTA: None of my friends feel that way.

OEDIPUS: But —

JOCASTA: From what I've heard, most men marry women who remind them of their mothers. So I figure why settle for second best when you can have the real thing?

OEDIPUS: But I can't have sex with you knowing — you're my mother.

JOCASTA: Not even on weekends?

OEDIPUS: No!

JOCASTA: I bet you want to do it with Helen, that Trojan slut, don't you?

OEDIPUS: No.

JOCASTA: Then who do you want to do it with?

OEDIPUS: I want to be with a woman to whom I'm not already related.

JOCASTA: I see. So now the whole family's not good enough to have sex with.

OEDIPUS: Will you be reasonable? I'm a public official. I'm a role model.

JOCASTA: So? Look at the Gods. The immortal Zeus has slept with his half-sister, his quarter-sister, his sixteenth-sister. If our own immortal gods get to boff their relatives, why can't you?

OEDIPUS: Because you're not just a relative, you're my mother!

JOCASTA: Must you make everything so complex, Oedipus?

OEDIPUS: Jocasta, this abomination against nature cannot continue.

JOCASTA: Look, Oedileh, I understand this is traumatic for you. But in a healthy marriage, you work through these things.

OEDIPUS: We don't have a healthy marriage!

JOCASTA: You want we should see a counselor?

OEDIPUS: No!

JOCASTA: Then what are you saying?

OEDIPUS: Mom . . . I want a divorce.

JOCASTA: *(Starts to cry hysterically.)* I never thought I'd hear such a thing from my own son.

Orange Lemon Egg Canary
Rinne Groff

Seriocomic

Great (thirties to forties); Trilby (twenties)

> This scene takes place in Great's apartment. Great is a professional
> magician. Trilby is a waitress who's his most recent sexual conquest.
> She is fascinated by magic. She has gone to one of his shows, where
> she saw him, afterwards, acting very friendly to another woman.

Great walks into his apartment wearing his suit. It is dark.

TRILBY: Welcome home.

GREAT: What the hell?

(Great turns on the light.)

GREAT: Shit, you scared me. How did you get in here?

TRILBY: Picked the lock.

GREAT: You what?

TRILBY: Bribed the super.

GREAT: Trilby.

TRILBY: He recognized me as your girlfriend and let me in. Is that so nuts?

GREAT: What are you doing here?

TRILBY: You're not happy to see me?

GREAT: Of course. How did you get in really?

TRILBY: Magic. I appeared here. Speaking of magic, did you have a good
show?

GREAT: Fine.

(Great comes over to kiss her; she pushes him away.)

TRILBY: You smell like lemons.

GREAT: What?

TRILBY: You stink. Have you been drinking?

GREAT: I had a couple drinks.

TRILBY: A couple drinks.

GREAT: I was performing.

TRILBY: What tricks did you pull?

GREAT: What do you mean?

TRILBY: What'd you perform tonight?

GREAT: The usual stuff.

(Trilby picks up a deck of cards.)

TRILBY: Pick a card, any card?

GREAT: Sort of.

(Trilby mocks Great's act using the card deck.)

TRILBY: Here's the Queen. But it's not the Queen, it's just a bunch of bullshit. See, it crosses the line that you made up in your head, and it
all turns to shit. I'm smarter than you, I'm better than you.

(Throwing the deck at him.)

I hate you.

GREAT: You saw my show.

TRILBY: Yeah, I saw your show all right. I waited outside her door for two
hours.

GREAT: It's not what you think it is. It's different than you think.

TRILBY: Oh excuse me, were you on the other side of the line? Stay away
from me. You probably have herpes. I wish you had herpes. I bet
you picked up herpes from one of those girls you screw after your
shows.

GREAT: I'm sorry that you had to see that.

TRILBY: Sorry that I saw or sorry that you did?

GREAT: I'm sorry. But we never said . . .

TRILBY: . . . that we wouldn't hurt and humiliate each other?

GREAT: It meant nothing. I thought of you.

TRILBY: Gross. Gross.

GREAT: Trilby.

TRILBY: Egypt warned me. I should have listened. I'm a moron.

GREAT: Don't say that.

TRILBY: A moron, an idiot, a retard. I'm a retard. Why should you feel
bad about lying to a retard?

GREAT: Please stop.

TRILBY: I wish I'd never walked through this door.

GREAT: Wait, stop, wait. I love you.

(Pause.)

TRILBY: How many times have you lied straight to my face?

GREAT: I don't want you to leave.

TRILBY: How could you do it? I couldn't even do it. My body couldn't. And don't give me the it's-the-act-you-don't-ask-why bullshit. There's a why. You do this to someone you love, you say you love.

GREAT: I love.

TRILBY: You learn it from your grandfather? Long line of magicians hurting women.

GREAT: It's got nothing to do with that.

TRILBY: It does: your upbringing, your models.

GREAT: My father wasn't a magician. He sold appliances.

TRILBY: Same difference. You're cursed.

GREAT: Nobody's cursed.

TRILBY: Cursed to repeat the same old tricks.

GREAT: It won't happen again.

TRILBY: How can I believe you if you don't even ask why?

GREAT: You don't want to hear why.

TRILBY: Don't tell me what I want.

Pathetic as I am, I think I cared more about the fact that that stupid perky imbecile gets to watch your shows whenever she wants, and me, I have to sneak in. She knows more about your magic than I do.

GREAT: All she knows is an act.

TRILBY: Your act. You.

GREAT: No.

TRILBY: You make her more important than me.

GREAT: Nothing's more important than you.

TRILBY: Another lie.

GREAT: What can I do to make you believe me?

TRILBY: Do you love me?

You said, I love you.

Do you love me?

Paradise
Chris Edmund

Dramatic

Clive (thirty, English); Amy (twenty-five, American)

Set in California. Clive and Amy have been having an affair. Clive has
decided to return to his partner in London.

CLIVE: I can't go through with it. *(Pause.)* I love you but I can't go on with
it. *(Pause.)* Well we own a house together. Julie and I have respon-
sibilities.

AMY: I don't believe this.

CLIVE: And other things.

AMY: What things?

CLIVE: Pressures.

AMY: Pressures?

CLIVE: Julie's sick.

AMY: Shame.

CLIVE: Amy, I'm in the wilderness.

AMY: And other cliches.

CLIVE: I just need to go home . . .

AMY: I have no sympathy.

CLIVE: Help me.

AMY: No.

CLIVE: Fuck you then.

AMY: I've heard of crazy reasons for not splitting up but a fucking house!

CLIVE: There's more to it than that but I've made up my mind.

AMY: Hey great!

CLIVE: Yes.

AMY: You made up your little mind!

CLIVE: Yes.

AMY: Don't you love me?

CLIVE: Yes I do.

AMY: Well then?

CLIVE: I can't.

AMY: Not love, a house. You're in the right country with the right president for this shit.

CLIVE: Absurd isn't it?

AMY: Fucking A it's absurd.

CLIVE: Amy.

AMY: Clive.

CLIVE: I'm sorry.

AMY: Yes you're sorry you jerk. Sorry again. All that British shit I'm sorry for this. I'm sorry for that. Sorry I fucked you but now I just have to fuck off so sorry . . . Sorry isn't feelings it's a cover up for feelings. You're not capable of feelings . . . I regret kissing you, I regret fucking you. I regret the blood on the sheets and gazing at you and regret telling you I love you.

CLIVE: Amy.

AMY: You know where I was at Thanksgiving?

CLIVE: Band practice.

AMY: I was having an abortion.

CLIVE: Liar.

AMY: Truth.

CLIVE: Bollocks.

AMY: Oh yeah, buddy.

CLIVE: Why?

AMY: Because I knew this day would come. In my heart I knew, Clive. There's a coldness in you that told me. It can be like a knife.

CLIVE: And other cliches.

AMY: You're an observer of life you don't *experience* it and nothing can touch you.

CLIVE: I think you should leave now.

AMY: I'm not finished yet.

CLIVE: Get out.

AMY: User. User!

CLIVE: You user. How could you?

AMY: Easy.

CLIVE: Like breaking an egg. Get out!

AMY: Look at me. Who do you see? Who do you see? *(Pause.)* You'll never, never understand.

CLIVE: Probably not. Bye bye.

AMY: Never.

CLIVE: Bye.

Playing House
Brooke Berman

Comic

Cory (late twenties); David (late twenties)

> Cory and David are married — for his green card. He's gay, she's
> straight. They've been living together since college — with their other
> best friend, a free spirited young massage therapist named June.

David and Cory having dinner. He's set the table with candles and wine
and flowers.

DAVID: Let's talk.

CORY: Sure.

DAVID: I'll go first.

CORY: Sure.

DAVID: I've been thinking about us. You and me.

CORY: Oh?

DAVID: It's complicated.

CORY: *(You noticed, huh?)* Yeah.

DAVID: You're my best friend.

CORY: You're mine too. And June.

DAVID: Oh, yeah, and June. Me too.

> *(Beat.)*

> You're always here for me. And June, too. When she's not acting out.

CORY: You're always here for me, too. And June too. I don't think she's
acting out.

DAVID: And, I want to kiss you. I've been thinking about that. What do
you think about that?

CORY: I missed something.

DAVID: Are you in love with me?

CORY: No, of course not. Why would you think that?

DAVID: Well, you just . . . I mean if you were, would you tell me? You
would, you'd tell me, wouldn't you tell me?

CORY: No. I would probably not tell you.

DAVID: So are you?

CORY: Am I what?

DAVID: You know.

CORY: I'm not.

DAVID: I am. With you.

CORY: You are?

DAVID: Yeah. It makes NO sense. But, yeah.

CORY: OK, I lied. I am too.

DAVID: So I want to.

CORY: You want to what?

DAVID: Kiss you.

CORY: That's weird.

DAVID: Why is it weird?

CORY: You like boys.

DAVID: I know. I still like boys. And, I want to kiss you.

CORY: No.

(They move toward each other.)

CORY: OK, yes. I think about things . . . touching you.

(The following is strange, awkward, delicate —)

DAVID: Touching me where?

(She smiles and points. She points to his throat, his wrists, his mouth.)

DAVID: We *are* married . . .

(She nods. They get closer.)

DAVID: I love you too. Like I don't love anyone. It's weird and strange and complicated, but I love you and trust you and need you — so why wouldn't you be the person I kiss? Well, OK, you're a girl and that counts you out, but why? Why, if you're the person I love?

CORY: *(Cutting him off with her lines, making him be quiet and just kiss her.)* SShh.

(They kiss again — this time very intensely. Eros.)

The Second String
Mac Rogers

Dramatic

Hannah (twenty-five to thirty-five); Piper (twenty-five to thirty-five)

> Hannah and Piper are a couple who have lived together for several
> years in New York City. Hannah has a high-powered career in finance
> and Piper teaches grade school. The scene takes place the second
> weekend after September 11, 2001. A college friend of theirs named
> Alan was killed in the World Trade Center attack and they spent the
> previous weekend at his funeral. This weekend they have returned
> to their college town somewhere in the South for their wedding. It
> had been set for this weekend for a year, and after an agonized dis-
> cussion, they've decided to go ahead with the ceremony as planned . . .
> until today, the day before the ceremony, when Piper says something
> unexpected.

HANNAH: OK what.

PIPER: What?

HANNAH: No, what. Tell me what. It's the ominous silence just before I'm
about to get in trouble for something I don't even know I've done
yet. Tell me what.

PIPER: Why aren't we talking about Alan?

HANNAH: Why aren't we talking about Alan? That's the thing?

PIPER: Why aren't we talking about him?

HANNAH: I don't understand — should we be talking about him?

PIPER: We've barely mentioned him all weekend.

HANNAH: That's all we talked about last weekend. We sat in circles, in,
in living rooms, "I'll never forget the time Alan," "my funniest memory of Alan," we sat in a church and listened to more people talk
about him.

PIPER: I just think it's strange that we're avoiding the subject.

HANNAH: I'm sorry, what are you saying we should do? Stare at his picture and cry? I miss him. I wish he was still here. I wish none of it

had ever happened. I mean Jesus, do you know anyone who doesn't wanna rewind the last three weeks?

PIPER: I feel like there's some kind of taboo.

HANNAH: This is our wedding! This is our weekend to do the most important thing we've ever done!

PIPER: And you don't want it messed up.

HANNAH: You know what? Let's call the guests. Let's call 'em. Let's call 'em and say, no wedding, no reception, no party, we're gonna sit around and remember Alan, who, by the way, none of us have actually forgotten. Oh — we've got caterers! They can walk around and serve food to the mourners!

PIPER: Hannah —

HANNAH: But I don't think that's what we're actually talking about, and I don't want to get ugly, but could we cut past the thing where I've done nothing wrong and you go ahead and tell me what I've really done wrong so I can do the doghouse and get back to the work I have to do?

PIPER: I hate you this way.

HANNAH: Well I hate you this way! Where I've gotta climb over a bunch of shit to find out what the real problem is, like we've got these infinite resources of time, like minutes aren't ticking away —

PIPER: Fucking bitch! *(Pause.)* Alan died. Alan was killed. We have to learn something from that.

HANNAH: Learn . . .

PIPER: I don't want to live in New York.

HANNAH: Wait, OK —

PIPER: I don't want to live there. It doesn't make sense, it's actually insane.

HANNAH: OK: You're bringing this up now?

PIPER: Deb and Michael said we could live with them.

HANNAH: You are kidding me.

PIPER: They have so much room —

HANNAH: You are kidding me. What right do they have?

PIPER: What are we proving —

HANNAH: What right do they have? Are they gonna take in everybody? All us helpless New Yorkers? Five to a room? Walk around ladling soup?

PIPER: What are we proving by living there?

HANNAH: That's our life, that's five years of my career, five brutal years —

PIPER: You've had to push so hard, is that really —

HANNAH: I like pushing hard! I like resistance, I want proof I did something! A woman, and a woman who's out, with all those guys, the ones who aren't condescending to me have these little movies playing in their heads, but whatever they are, in their field they're the best, I have to be working with the best, or what's the point?

PIPER: There's other points! We're talking about a lifetime — I mean, what is this for? You said to me: "I want to spend my life having stupid fights with you."

HANNAH: I mean it.

PIPER: I thought it was beautiful.

HANNAH: I want to fight over the chores, I wanna fight over the kids, I wanna pick at stupid little things, I want you to pick at stupid little things. I'd rather spend a lifetime fighting than have one minute of peace without you.

PIPER: I'm saying: You grew up in New York. That's your vision of life, it's struggle. But — I mean — look out the window — that's not the whole world. What if we could have both — a whole life, and peace? We're targets up there. That's what we know now, our lives are just something somebody in some other country is gonna make a point with. Why are we there? What's good about it?

HANNAH: I will not be chased out of my home.

PIPER: Well shit, if you have to look at it that way —

HANNAH: *We will not be chased out of our home!*

PIPER: WHOSE HOME? MY HOME?!

(*Silence.*)

HANNAH: I can't finish — I just can't finish this conversation. I can't finish this conversation now. Do you understand? I have to talk to Deb, I have to — this is insane. I have to talk to Deb.

PIPER: We have to solve this.

HANNAH: We will.

PIPER: We have to solve this. I'm over a barrel — I have to be with you.
(*Pause.*)

HANNAH: We're both over a barrel.

Temptation
David Kosh

Comic

Cybele and Leon (twenties)

> This scene is taken from a short satirical play about a put-upon office drone and a free-spirited temp who cross paths one day at a soulless workplace. Leon is a full-time collater at Scan, Collate, Copy, Inc. Cybele, the temp, helping Leon on a large rush job, believes everything has meaning and that she has been assigned to this awful job solely to meet Leon, who just might be her soul mate. Now she has to convince Leon. As for props — there should be a long table with stacks of paper situated on it, and two staplers.

LEON: This has to be done by five. The client's coming at five. Collated, stapled, and stacked. I'll show you . . . Watch me.

CYBELE: I think I can figure . . .

LEON: You don't know how easy it is to miss a page or get them out of order. And paper cuts. Paper cuts . . . You have to watch me . . . *(As Cybele smiles.)* . . . Do you know how much paper cuts hurt? This is serious. There was a collator once, working with eighty pound stock. Sliced his pinky to the bone, OK?

CYBELE: I'm sorry, Leon.

LEON: Right to the bone.

CYBELE: I'm sorry.

LEON: And on his way home from the hospital he was run over by an SUV. He's dead.

CYBELE: That's terrible.

LEON: Isn't it? So you take your first page. Then you take the second and slide it under the first. Gently. We don't want any crumples or wrinkles.

CYBELE: But crumples and wrinkles make life interesting. If everything in the world was smooth and shiny —

LEON: People have to read this, Cybele.

CYBELE: You pronounced it perfectly.

LEON: Soft *C*, accent on the last *E*. You take the third page and —

CYBELE: Cybele was an ancient nature goddess. Asia Minor. Great Mother and all that. Earth, moon, fertility. Worshiped on mountaintops. Bloody, orgiastic ceremonies. Pretty intense.

LEON: You take the third page and —

CYBELE: You're pretty intense too, Leon.

LEON: You take the third page and —

CYBELE: Oh, forget it . . . First page, second page, third page, fourth, fifth, sixth, etcetera, etcetera, all collated . . . *(Stapling the sheets.)*. . . Stapled . . . *(Tossing them on table.)* . . . And stacked.

LEON: Wow. You're good. You're just a temp, right?

CYBELE: I'm not "just" anything, Leon. There's a long list. Human being, woman, right-wing militia leader.

LEON: Really?

CYBELE: I'm kidding.

LEON: About which one?

CYBELE: You made a joke.

LEON: I know another one.

CYBELE: OK.

LEON: Why did the Eskimo see a psychiatrist?

CYBELE: Can I give you a note?

LEON: Huh?

CYBELE: They're Inuits. Use Inuit.

LEON: All right. Why did the Inuit see a psychiatrist?

CYBELE: I don't know. Why?

LEON: His parents are cold . . .

(As Cybele laughs.)

. . . You don't want my job, do you?

CYBELE: No, Leon, I don't.

LEON: OK. Good.

CYBELE: I don't want your job.

LEON: Great.

CYBELE: Not your job.

LEON: Great. Let's start, OK?

CYBELE: I dreamt about lions this morning.

LEON: What?

CYBELE: Lions. Leon.

LEON: I'm gonna get fired if we don't finish this.

CYBELE: What did you dream about?

LEON: The Matterhorn. I was on the Matterhorn. With Shirley Temple.

CYBELE: Temple on a mountaintop.

LEON: Covered in red.

CYBELE: Blood.

LEON: *Heidi* is my favorite movie.

CYBELE: Mine, too.

LEON: The Shirley Temple version? With Jean Hersholt as grandfather?

CYBELE: I love Jean Hersholt. He was such a humanitarian.

LEON: Colorized or black-and-white?

CYBELE: Black-and-white. Colorized is a crime against all that's good and decent.

LEON: Do you like pizza?

CYBELE: Green pepper anchovy.

(It's clear by Leon's expression that Cybele's choice of topping is also his. An indefinable something flashes between them. They move toward each other, then Leon rushes back to work.)

LEON: I'm gonna get fired.

CYBELE: OK . . . *(Picking up the first page.)* . . . Have you read this? Have you read any of this?

LEON: Are there typos?

CYBELE: I knew it.

LEON: The proofreaders are the worst.

CYBELE: There was something about the air this morning. The way it made my skin tingle when I stepped outside.

LEON: They drink vodka and pretend it's water.

CYBELE: I could smell it, too. And taste it. Today is a *day*.

LEON: And they're mean.

CYBELE: Leon . . .

LEON: Really mean.

CYBELE: Leon . . .

LEON: Drunk and mean.

CYBELE: Hey! . . . Look.

(She thrusts the first page at him. He reads.)

LEON: "Bert Lahr: A Munchkin Remembers."

(Cybele grins at Leon, but she gets no response.)

CYBELE: Bert Lahr . . . the Lion . . . *(Still no response.)* . . . Wizard of Oz!
Bert Lahr was the Lion. The Lion. There's meaning everywhere, isn't
that what I said? Even in a hell hole like this.

LEON: Hell hole? I don't think —

CYBELE: Close your eyes.

LEON: What?

CYBELE: Close your eyes! . . . Now see. See what you're seeing. Feel what
you're feeling.

LEON: I — I . . .

CYBELE: You can do this, Leon.

LEON: I see . . . I see . . .

CYBELE: Yes? Yes?

LEON: I see grass. Lots of grass. It's everywhere. And I see animals — ze-
bras, giraffes. They're running. Running from me.

CYBELE: How does that make you feel?

LEON: I feel . . . *(Growling.)* . . . I feel . . .

(Another growl — a little louder.)

CYBELE: You feel leonine, L-E-O-N-I-N-E. Of, relating to, suggestive of,
or resembling —

LEON: Bert Lahr!

CYBELE: No. Try again.

LEON: . . . A lion . . . a real lion.

CYBELE: Yes.

LEON: With really big teeth.

CYBELE: And sharp claws and a ferocious heart. A wild beast. Cybele was
goddess of wild beasts. And lions were her sacred animals. Are you
my sacred animal, Leon?

LEON: Roar.

CYBELE: Are you my wild beast?

LEON: *Roar!*

CYBELE: Are you my wild, sacred beast?

(Leon lets out a huge roar. Cybele grabs a piece of paper from one of the stacks and slices it across her palm.)

CYBELE: Then drink the blood of Cybele!

LEON: A paper cut. Oh my God.

CYBELE: Drink it.

LEON: Oh my God.

CYBELE: Drink it!

LEON: Oh my Goddess.

(He lunges at her palm, licking, slurping, biting.)

CYBELE: I am the Moon and the Earth and you are the Beast. Divinity manifests through our union and the power of the universe explodes in our loins, oh take me, take me, Sacred Beast.

(Another savage roar from Leon.)

CYBELE: Take me now!

(One more roar and Leon shoves the stacks of paper on the floor, then sweeps Cybele off her feet and deposits her on the table.)

CYBELE: Purrrr . . .

Three Prayers
Greg Zittel

Dramatic

Bill and Molley (both teens)

> Bill's dad runs a saloon. He has come over to Molley's house to tell her that her mother is over there, misbehaving.

MOLLEY: *(To Bill.)* I'm sorry.

BILL: About what?

MOLLEY: What can I do for you?

BILL: Nuthin' for me.

MOLLEY: Why are you here?

BILL: Your ma is at my dad's saloon.

MOLLEY: Is she bad?

BILL: Uh-huh.

> *(Molley walks to her table, pulls her rosary from apron pocket, and sits. She blesses herself and begins praying.)*

BILL: Uhhhhh, whaddaya want me to do?

MOLLEY: I don't know.

BILL: She's pretty drunk.

MOLLEY: I know.

BILL: *(Ill at ease.)* Would you quit praying a minute and talk to me?

MOLLEY: I'm sorry, but I don't know what to do.

BILL: Talk to me.

MOLLEY: She gets drunk more and more lately. She lets the house go when she gets like this. I'm becoming a mother to my younger brother and I don't know what to do anymore so I have to pray.

BILL: You're in a fix.

MOLLEY: It's awful I'm telling you.

> *(She puts her head in her hands and begins to cry.)*

BILL: *(Pause. Then, he walks to her.)* Uhhhh.

MOLLEY: *(Searches.)* I need a handkerchief.

BILL: I ain't got one.

MOLLEY: I'm sixteen now and I guess I better think about getting a job.

BILL: They're hard to find.

MOLLEY: I know.

BILL: Ain't your father workin'?

MOLLEY: *(Starts crying again.)* Ohhh.

BILL: What?

MOLLEY: It's OK.

BILL: You're crying.

MOLLEY: I'm OK.

BILL: What's the matter?

MOLLEY: I've got to get a job.

BILL: What about your old man?

MOLLEY: He's gone a week now.

BILL: Oh.

MOLLEY: I heard the phone company is hiring.

BILL: Where'd he go?

MOLLEY: Just gone.

BILL: He didn't go lookin' for work?

MOLLEY: He drank, too.

BILL: I drink, I'm here.

MOLLEY: *(Confronts him.)* You drink?

BILL: Yeah, sure.

MOLLEY: Don't drink.

BILL: I don't get drunk.

MOLLEY: Everybody drinks gets drunk.

BILL: No. I don't get drunk.

MOLLEY: You swear?

BILL: *(He thinks about this.)* No.

MOLLEY: I think you should leave.

BILL: What about your mother?

MOLLEY: It doesn't matter. She doesn't cause trouble and I've got to clean up this place. She made a mess and then left it and went out drinking.

BILL: You just gonna leave her at the saloon?

MOLLEY: Yes!

BILL: I'm sorry.

MOLLEY: It's not your fault.

BILL: Well hell, it seems every time I say something you either argue, cry, or get all angry.

MOLLEY: I'm not angry at you.

BILL: I think you're pretty.

MOLLEY: Oh, Jesus.

BILL: Hum . . . I think you're the prettiest girl in the whole high school.

MOLLEY: I think you better start praying to Saint Anthony.

BILL: Why?

MOLLEY: *(Flattered, enjoying him.)* You lost your marbles.

BILL: What?

MOLLEY: You're goofy and I've got things to do.

BILL: Lemme help.

MOLLEY: No no.

BILL: Come on.

MOLLEY: No. Now you should go.

BILL: Hey look. How about if I go and get your mom and bring her back here?

MOLLEY: No.

BILL: I'll carry her if I have to.

MOLLEY: No damn it. Now stop.

BILL: I'm sorry.

MOLLEY: *(Crying.)* Just go please.

BILL: OK. *(He goes to the door and waits.)* Uhhh . . . My name is Dunphy. I'm ol' Bill Dunphy's oldest. I'm Bill Dunphy. They named me after my ol' man. I'm gonna take over the saloon some day. I'll make somebody a good husband and I'd like it OK if it was you.

MOLLEY: *(Shocked.)* What?

BILL: I wanna marry you.

MOLLEY: You're crazy.

BILL: I do.

MOLLEY: Go on. You got bats in your belfry.

BILL: I know you think I'm a noodnick but I been watchin' you at least a year now.

MOLLEY: What?

BILL: You walk by the saloon doncha?

MOLLEY: You watch?

BILL: When you go to school you walk by Dunphy's right?

MOLLEY: Yeah.

BILL: Well, half the time I'm watchin ya.

MOLLEY: Well, that's not very nice.

BILL: Why not?

MOLLEY: Good people don't sit around watching other people.

BILL: You walk with your friend the little kid.

MOLLEY: She's short, she's not little.

BILL: Alright, the short kid.

MOLLEY: She's my friend. She's not a kid. A kid is a goat.

BILL: OK. OK. Your friend. The short one, right?

MOLLEY: She's four feet eleven inches.

BILL: Oh Jeez. She stopped growin' too, it looks. I mean over the past year she's about the same height now as she was last year.

MOLLEY: Yes, I think she stopped growing.

BILL: Do you have a nickname for her?

MOLLEY: A nickname?

BILL: Yeah.

MOLLEY: No.

BILL: You don't?

MOLLEY: No.

BILL: How come?

MOLLEY: How come?

BILL: Yeah.

MOLLEY: Why should I have a nickname for her?

BILL: Cause she's so short.

MOLLEY: No, her name is Mae and that's what I call her.

BILL: Doncha find it kinda funny when you're with somebody that small?

MOLLEY: *(Enjoying him.)* No, and I might tell you it's no way to impress me by telling me you think my friends are strange.

BILL: No, I didn't say strange. No, uh-huh, not strange.

MOLLEY: OK.

BILL: Short.

MOLLEY: *(Enjoying this.)* OK, that's enough.

BILL: And I just think you're missin' a great opportunity to give some-body a nickname.

MOLLEY: Why should anybody have a nickname?

BILL: It's fun. My friend Ted is "Pee-Wee" and my friend Eddie Flanagan is "Squatty-body" cause he's so short and stocky and my friend Mike is called "Derbo" because he's so dirty.

MOLLEY: How do you get Derbo out of the fact that he's dirty?

BILL: Well, everybody used to call him "Dirt" and then dirt got to be "Derbo."

MOLLEY: Why?

BILL: I dunno. It just happened that way.

MOLLEY: I don't get it.

BILL: It's just more interesting when everybody has a nickname. I know a guy "Itsey-Boy" and I'll bet you, you couldn't find a person alive who knows what his real name is.

MOLLEY: Is he short because it would make sense if he was short and called "Itsey" like "Itsey-Bitsey" means a little piece of candy or something.

BILL: Itsey-Boy? Heck no, he's a big guy and getting' bigger. I'll bet he weighs a ton and he's a real kibitzer, you know the type?

MOLLEY: Yes, and I don't like the type, either.

BILL: Oh yeah. I can see your point.

(Pause.)

MOLLEY: I have work to do here.

BILL: Yeah. I guess I better go.

MOLLEY: Yes.

BILL: You gonna clean up, huh?

MOLLEY: Yes.

BILL: I'd offer to help but I'm no good at housework and stuff.

MOLLEY: That's OK.

BILL: I'll be more help looking after your ma till you get there.

MOLLEY: I have a novena I say at home that I think I'll say before I clean up and come over.

BILL: My dad says prayin' don't help.

MOLLEY: Your dad's a drunk.

BILL: Well . . . no.

MOLLEY: He's a drunk and he runs a saloon.

BILL: *(Straightforward.)* He drinks and he runs a saloon.

MOLLEY: God!

BILL: That don't make him wrong though.

MOLLEY: I hate alcohol and that's what you mean to me. I wish my mother would never set foot in that place.

BILL: I'm sorry you feel that way.

MOLLEY: *(Softens to him.)* That's OK, it's not your fault.
    (Pause.)

BILL: Could I kiss you before I go?

MOLLEY: *(Thinks.)* OK..
    (Bill walks to her. They kiss gently for some time. Her hand touches his face.)

BILL: Thanks.

MOLLEY: *(Worried.)* Is that a sin?

BILL: Did ya think anything dirty when ya did it?

MOLLEY: *(Definite.)* No.

BILL: Then I don't see no reason why it would be a sin.

MOLLEY: No?

BILL: Do you?

MOLLEY: Uhn-uh.

BILL: Well then?

MOLLEY: I guess you're right.

BILL: Anyways my dad says there ain't no such thing as sin.

MOLLEY: No?

BILL: Uhn-uh.

MOLLEY: Then how come everybody's going to confession?

BILL: I don't know, I'll ask my dad.
    (Molley, almost dancing, moves to look outside.)

MOLLEY: I think it's raining. *(Looks.)* It is.

BILL: Hard?

MOLLEY: Yes. Did you bring an umbrella?

BILL: No.
    (She folds laundry.)

MOLLEY: I don't have one to give you.

BILL: *(Makes a muscle.)* I don't need no umbrella.

MOLLEY: *(Smiles.)* I could give you some newspaper.

BILL: *(Pause.)* I don't read.

MOLLEY: To put over your head so you don't get wet.

BILL: Oh.

    (They laugh.)

MOLLEY: I don't want you to catch cold.

BILL: What kind a' malarkey is that? I can stand a little rain.

MOLLEY: *(Looking at him.)* I like you.

BILL: Can I come back?

MOLLEY: *(Puts down the laundry.)* Yes, but I don't want to kiss for awhile.

BILL: What'll we do?

MOLLEY: We can go for walks.

BILL: Ah, yeah. We could do that.

MOLLEY: Talk.

BILL: OK.

MOLLEY: I'd like that.

BILL: It's a deal.

MOLLEY: I'm glad you came over. I don't know what I'm going to do about my mom, but you've made it a nicer day.

BILL: That's good.

MOLLEY: Bye.

Tristan
Don Nigro

Dramatic

Matt (midthirties); Alison (nineteen)

> Matt Armitage is the lawyer for the Rose family of east Ohio, and
> for years he's been secretly looking after Fay Morgan, a troubled
> woman, once a servant for the Roses, and the mother of Alison by
> Gavin Rose's father, John Pendragon. But now, in the autumn of
> 1887, Fay has died, making Alison swear to return to Ohio and claim
> her rightful inheritance. When Alison shows up in a rainstorm, pre-
> tending not to know her name or where she's come from, the Rose
> family takes her in, and their son, Rhys, falls in love with her. His
> father Gavin suspects strongly who Alison is, but he has so far not
> acknowledged this, which puts Matt in a terrible position. He does-
> n't know whether to reveal Alison's secret or not. He wants to pro-
> tect the family, but he also loves Alison, and he wants no harm to
> come to her. Alison knows that Matt, a good and happily married
> man, can't help desiring her, and although she's fond of him, and in-
> creasingly fond of the Roses themselves, she's quite willing to black-
> mail him into keeping silent until she can figure out what she wants.
> Matt finds her walking by the pond at the Pendragon house and is
> determined to do the right thing. He just isn't yet clear what it is.

Alison walks by the pond, evening. Bird sounds. Matt at his desk.
MATT: All day my mind was full of her. Drink, as usual, was no help. What
  did she think she was doing? I didn't take the train to Maryland. *(He
  begins to move toward Alison.)* Instead, in the evening I went out to
  the Pendragon house, and found her walking alone by the pond.
ALISON: Hello, Matt. I knew you'd come. Thank you for not telling.
MATT: What are you doing here?
ALISON: I've come home.
MATT: Do you know how worried your sister's been?

ALISON: She knew this is where I'd be.

MATT: How could you run off and leave her to deal with your mother's death all by herself?

ALISON: My sister is a very resourceful person. She'll do fine. When Mother died, I just got on a train and came. I promised her I would, and that's what I did.

MATT: What do you think you're going to accomplish here?

ALISON: I don't know. I like it here. At least, I think I do. The people more than the house, which is odd, because Mother always led me to believe the house would be wonderful and the people horrible, but it seems to me to be just the opposite. The house scares me, but I feel very close to the people, the town, the woods and the pond and everything. I feel like I belong here.

MATT: This is not where you belong right now.

ALISON: It's exactly where I belong. It's my home.

MATT: That's your mother talking, not you.

ALISON: My mother is gone. And I've come home. That's all there is to it. You won't tell them who I am, will you? I think Gavin knows, but he hasn't said anything. I thought the first thing he'd do might be to contact you and try and get you to take me back to Maryland, but he hasn't done that, has he?

MATT: I haven't spoken to him.

ALISON: I'm sure he knows. He recognized me the minute he saw me. I look like my mother.

MATT: Yes, you do. Very much.

ALISON: But he hasn't said. Why hasn't he said?

MATT: Gavin is a very private man, and most of his life he's preferred not to know things.

ALISON: But he does know.

MATT: Then he prefers not to say. You put me in a very awkward position here. Gavin has always supplied the money to support you and your mother and sister —

ALISON: To pay us, for taking care of the house in Maryland. Don't make it sound like charity.

MATT: But he made my father promise never to mention anything about you to him.

ALISON: Why would he do that?

MATT: Partly I think he didn't want to upset Bel. She's not a person you want to get upset. And he just didn't want to think about it any more. Your mother was pregnant with you when she left, and Bel had a serious breakdown after what happened here. So my father handled it all for Gavin, and when my father died, I took over, and all these years Gavin hasn't said two words to me about it.

ALISON: So for all he knows, you could be robbing him blind.

MATT: He knows I'm not robbing him. We keep very complete records. He's looked at the books. I'm sure he's aware of every time you had a doctor bill or anything else. We just don't talk about it. That's his way.

ALISON: So now that I've shown up here, you don't know whether to come right out and tell him it's me, or just keep your mouth shut like he told you to. How will he find out my mother's dead? Come across the funeral expenses in your damned account books?

MATT: That's entirely possible.

ALISON: I think that's a really sick way to live.

MATT: And how would you characterize what you're doing?

ALISON: What do you think I'm doing?

MATT: I don't know what you're doing. Do you?

ALISON: Do you want me to just come out and tell everybody, to make things easier for you? Because I don't particularly care to make things easy for you. If Gavin doesn't want to talk about it, then it seems to me I should do him the courtesy of not forcing the issue.

MATT: What you should do is go home.

ALISON: I AM home. *(Pause.)* You've always been a good friend to me. I always look forward to you and your father coming to Maryland, to the books you'd bring me, to playing chess with you. And you were kind to my mother, even when she wasn't always very nice to you. I don't want to cause you any trouble, I really don't. But I'm not going back.

MATT: Then what are you going to do?

ALISON: I haven't decided yet. I want to get to know them a little better first. After all, they are my family.

MATT: Alison, I can't let you hurt these people. You know that.

ALISON: What do you think I'm going to do with them? Kill them? A sweet, innocent little creature like me?

MATT: I'm going to have to speak to Gavin about it.

ALISON: You're not going to tell him, Matt. You know you're not.

MATT: Why aren't I?

ALISON: Because you're in love with me.

MATT: What kind of thing is that to say?

ALISON: A true thing. I know you people like to avoid the truth as much as possible, but my mother taught me to look with a cold eye and see what's there, and the truth is, you've been in love with me for a long time.

MATT: I'm married.

ALISON: Exactly.

MATT: Just what is that supposed to mean?

ALISON: You won't tell because you're in love with me, and because Gavin doesn't want to know, and because he already knows, and because if you do, I'll tell your wife about us.

MATT: Tell her what about us?

ALISON: That you're in love with me and you've been sneaking off to Maryland to see me for some years now.

MATT: My wife knows I go to Maryland.

ALISON: Does she know why?

MATT: I have no secrets from my wife.

ALISON: You've got one.

MATT: I don't know what you're talking about.

ALISON: What about when you held me in the chapel behind the house?

MATT: You were upset because your mother was dying. You were crying. What was I supposed to do?

ALISON: You wanted me.

MATT: I was comforting a person I've known since she was a child.

ALISON: I am not a child, and you desired me at that moment.

MATT: I pitied you.

ALISON: And you wanted me. Can you stand there and deny it? You're a fairly honest man, for a lawyer, and you know it's true. So I don't think you're going to say anything to anybody about me, are you?

MATT: If you're under the impression I'm going to let you blackmail me over something that didn't even happen, you're very much mistaken.

ALISON: Please, Matt. I don't want to fight with you. I just want some time to get to know my family. Just give me a little time with them. I think maybe that's why Gavin hasn't said anything. He needs time, so we can get to know each other. You've got a family. You've got a wife and a little boy. Just let me know my family. I don't want to hurt anybody here. I swear I don't. Maybe it won't work out. Maybe I'll just go away and never tell them, but I've got to spend some time with them first. Don't I have a right to do that?

MATT: I'm going to Maryland tomorrow, to help your sister take care of things there. Why don't you come with me?

ALISON: I've got things to do here.

MATT: Alison, it's your mother.

ALISON: I know it's my mother. I'm doing what my mother wanted.

MATT: That's what scares me.

ALISON: How about this: You go to Maryland for a few days and get everything settled there, make sure Holly's all right. Let me stay here and get to know my family. Just don't mention it to Gavin before you leave. Is that too much to ask? You'll be doing your job. Gavin will have some time to bring it up himself if he wants to. Then when you get back we'll talk. Will you just give me that?

MATT: You really should come with me.

ALISON: I'm not going with you.

(Pause.)

MATT: All right. I'll give you a few days. But when I get back here, we're going to deal with this. And there's something you and I have got to get straight right now. Nothing has ever happened between us, and nothing ever will. I have a wife and a child that I love very much, and there never was and never will be anything between you and me. Is that clear?

ALISON: I would never want to do anything to hurt you, Matt. Or your wife, or your little boy. You're a very good friend of mine. I know I can always count on you. It's really an enormous comfort to me knowing that whatever happens, I can always count on you. Thank you. *(She kisses him on the cheek, but it's not exactly an innocent kiss. He looks at her. Then he turns and goes. Alison looks after him. Bird sounds.)*

The Wax
Kathleen Tolan

Seriocomic

Maureen and Hal (forties)

> Maureen and Hal, in their forties, were married and are now separated. Today, at a gathering of old friends for a wedding, is the first they've seen each other since they split and Hal took up with Ben. Hal was a brilliant, rising star, classical composer who never fulfilled his promise. His memoir has just been published. Theirs was a volatile and loving relationship. Maureen was a dancer. She makes hairpin turns from love to vindictiveness and back. She needs completion with Hal. Earlier this evening they found themselves alone for a moment and fell into a passionate embrace. Now, inadvertently, they have been left alone, again, in a friend's hotel room. Maureen plays music to calm herself. Hal has just taken a shower to wash off the sloe gin fizz Maureen dumped on him earlier.

Maureen turns on the boom box. "Que Faro" from Gluck's "Orfeo ed Euridice" is sung. Maureen lies back on the pillows, closes her eyes, and breathes deeply. Hal comes in from the bathroom wrapped in a towel, sees Maureen on the bed, looks around, realizes they're alone. Careful not to disturb her, he goes over to Christopher's suitcase and rifles through it. He takes out some pajamas and a hairbrush falls to the floor making a clunk. Maureen jolts up.

MAUREEN: What are you doing?

(He pulls on the pajamas.)

HAL: Nothing. Go back to sleep.

MAUREEN: I wasn't sleeping.

HAL: That's Gluck.

MAUREEN: Excuse me?

HAL: *(Sings.)* "Che faro senza Euridice . . ." He's lost her.

MAUREEN: How tragic for him.

HAL: He looked back.

MAUREEN: Big mistake.

HAL: Maureen, I'm sorry, I'm sorry, I didn't mean —

(Maureen turns off the tape.)

MAUREEN: Spit it out, Hal.

HAL: You kissed me. And I responded. I don't want to give you the wrong impression.

MAUREEN: Gee, Hal, don't worry. I got the wrong impression long before that kiss.

HAL: Oh. Right.

MAUREEN: It meant nothing.

HAL: I knew that.

MAUREEN: I was just embracing the paradox. I was fucking with your head.

HAL: Well, thanks.

MAUREEN: Come here.

HAL: What for?

MAUREEN: Just come here.

HAL: No.

MAUREEN: I dare you.

HAL: All right.

(He goes to her. She kisses him. It becomes passionate.)

HAL: Oh, Maureen.

(Maureen pulls back.)

MAUREEN: You slut.

HAL: I know.

(They embrace, full of feeling.)

MAUREEN: How could you write a *memoir* and say *nothing* about this, about us, about floating down our muddy river on our tube, do you remember that?

HAL: Yes.

MAUREEN: The weeds, the rocks, the gentle current pulling us along —

HAL: Yes

MAUREEN: Pulling you up on the bank, sliding on the bank, the mud, sliding on the mud —

HAL: Yes

MAUREEN: Taking you on the mud —

HAL: Oh, Maureen, Maureen —

MAUREEN: Having you on the mud, the slime, and then, with the frogs, the fish, in the shade of the birds and branches —

HAL: *(The memory is too painful.)* Please, don't, Maureen, really, no need to bring up the muck —

MAUREEN: You sang to me.

HAL: No.

MAUREEN: Your music. Your most beautiful music.

HAL: No.

MAUREEN: I miss it. Just once, now, one more time, before the others come. *(Hal sings. Maureen harmonizes. It's a beautiful, atonal, eerie work.)*

HAL: I do miss you, Maureen, and the mud, the silt, the squall and squander and decay that was our life

MAUREEN: *(Sudden rage.)* And you gave that up to write cheap *fiction* and hang out at the *gay bars* with your *critic?!*

HAL: *(Furious.)* See! You are homophobic.

MAUREEN: And you're a moron.

HAL: What are you, my mother?

MAUREEN: I should be your mother. I'd slap you around.

HAL: You're the one who started fucking around, Maureen. I really don't know how you get to assume the mantle of the wounded martyr when it was you —

MAUREEN: You wouldn't have me.

HAL: Well I would in my way. You started watching those talk shows, reading those self-help books, you decided that what we had wasn't enough.

MAUREEN: OK, I got this thing that I wanted to be plowed, penetrated, OK, so maybe I shouldn't have taken it literally.

HAL: Well it's over, OK? But if I ever write a "novel" again I assure you I'll put you in. And, damn it, why don't you write your own damn novel. Did you ever think of that?

MAUREEN: Well, maybe I will.

HAL: Good.

MAUREEN: Maybe I just Goddamn will.

HAL: Great.

MAUREEN: You love me, admit it.

HAL: Fine. I love my mother. That doesn't mean I want to live with her. And what's it to you, anyway? Do you want me? Do you really want me?

MAUREEN: I want to take you, use you, spit you out, and discard you.

HAL: Gee, that sounds like fun.

MAUREEN: *(She begins to cry.)* I want you . . . I want you to remember me.

HAL: *(Moved.)* I'm sorry. I am sorry, Maureen. Of course I remember you. How could I not?

(They hold and comfort each other. The door knob rattles. They freeze, panic, rush to hide. Maureen hides in the closet. Hal grabs his pajama top and dives under the bed.)

Scenes for
Two Women

All Cotton
Shel Silverstein

Comic

Rachel and Jill (could be any age)

> Rachel is a sales clerk in a small boutique. Jill bought a blouse there a few days previously. It was supposed to be a "no-shrink" blouse; but it has shrunk. This has really pissed her off, and she's returned to the boutique, whose policy is to disallow returns, to demand that they make an exception in this case; but Rachel is adamant about upholding the store's policy. Which pisses Jill off even more.

> *Monique's Boutique. A sign says "All Cotton." Another says "All Sales Final — No Refunds." Jill stands looking at sign over blouses. Rachel approaches her.*

JILL: These are all cotton?

RACHEL: One-hundred-percent combed cotton. We have them in some great colors. But I like the white best.

JILL: The shrinkage — that's what I'm thinking about.

RACHEL: It's nonshrink.

JILL: Guaranteed.

RACHEL: Absolutely. What are you, a five? *(She starts toward rack.)* I can show you the colors we have left —

JILL: I can show you — *(She opens jacket.)* this — *(She is wearing a tiny shrunken blouse.)*

RACHEL: What is that? Is that one of *ours?*

JILL: Non-shrink — one-hundred-percent cotton — the same blouse — guaranteed.

RACHEL: What size is that? If that's a *three* you can't expect —

JILL: Why would I buy a three? So I could look ridiculous and be uncomfortable? It's a *nine* — check the size.

RACHEL: *(Looking at size tag.)* Size — nine — boy, did that shrink. What did you wash it in?

JILL: Boiling chicken soup. What do you think I washed it in?

RACHEL: I've never seen *anything* shrink like that.

JILL: I washed it in cold water, gentle detergent — by *hand*.

RACHEL: Sometimes the *dryer* can . . .

JILL: Dripped *dry* — I wouldn't put a forty-dollar blouse in a dryer.

RACHEL: Well, *something* shrunk the heck out of it.

JILL: *Something* like the cotton itself.

RACHEL: *Maybe.*

JILL: What *else?*

RACHEL: I don't know.

JILL: Well — I'm returning it — *(Takes it off.)*

RACHEL: *(Looking at tag.)* You're sure you got this here? I don't remember having this color.

JILL: You want to see the receipt?

RACHEL: No, it's not that I doubt you — I just don't remember seeing this color —

JILL: It *was* brighter.

RACHEL: Well I will need the receipt. The boss insists that I — *(Jill hands her the receipt.)* Uh — who waited on you? I don't recognize this . . .

JILL: Are you suggesting that — somebody snuck in here — and sold me this shrinky, fadey blouse — without your permission?

RACHEL: I was only —

JILL: Well, what do you mean, who waited on me? A short women with red hair.

RACHEL: *Red* hair?

JILL: Reddish — yes.

RACHEL: And this was . . . *(Looks.)* when?

JILL: Tuesday — or Wednesday — it should say on the receipt.

RACHEL: Well, whoever it was didn't write the date. Probably Roxanne.

JILL: *Probably* Roxanne? Roxanne has red hair?

RACHEL: Roxanne's hair changes daily . . . All right — I can give you another blouse — or credit on any other item — except for the jewelry.

JILL: By another blouse — you mean, another style?

RACHEL: This is the only style — on sale — I can't give you a nonsale item.

JILL: You mean I can have another of the guaranteed nonshrink blouses.

RACHEL: Well, sometimes *one* individual blouse will shrink — out of an entire shipment.

JILL: It's the cotton — if they're all the same cotton, they're all going to shrink.

RACHEL: Well, I can credit you toward any other sale item.

JILL: What I'd like is my money back. I'd like the forty-two fifty.

RACHEL: I can't do that — *(Points to sign.)* I can apply the purchase price toward any item of lesser or comparable —

JILL: You said *guaranteed.*

RACHEL: It is guaranteed — if it *wasn't* guaranteed we wouldn't credit the purchase price toward another item, would we?

JILL: *Guarantee* doesn't mean giving one credit toward another blouse of equal shrink potential —

RACHEL: Or toward any other nonsale item.

JILL: But this is the only sale item — apart from the jewelry.

RACHEL: I can't credit this toward jewelry.

JILL: Well — there you are — or here I am —

RACHEL: I wish I could do more for you.

JILL: You're not doing *anything* for me. You're offering me another useless blouse in return for *this* useless blouse.

RACHEL: This is not my shop. I am not Monique.

JILL: Oh. "This is not my shop — I'm not Monique" — so anything goes.

RACHEL: They do guarantee their products — based upon —

JILL: Oh *they* guarantee — *their* products — a minute ago it was *we* guarantee — When I first walked in it was *I* guarantee — We're going backwards.

RACHEL: I can only do what I can do.

JILL: And I'll do what I can do.

RACHEL: I only work here.

JILL: You're — asking for trouble.

RACHEL: You can come back. The owner will be in on Wednesday — or Thursday.

JILL: Can you give the owner's phone number? Monique's? I suppose you can't.

RACHEL: I can take *your* number and have *her* reach *you.*

JILL: Uh-huh — but you're not giving me my money back.

RACHEL: I can't do that — *(Points to sign.)*

JILL: All right — I've been very — civilized with you. And I'm not a civilized person — not in *your* sense of the word.

RACHEL: I can't do something that I can't do.

JILL: I can do things — *(She leans toward Rachel.)*

RACHEL: What?

JILL: *Things* — things you don't want me to do.

RACHEL: Don't start any trouble in here.

JILL: I'm going to start trouble in here — I'm going to *make* trouble — *brew* trouble.

RACHEL: You'll get arrested.

JILL: For what? I'm not going to start any *fires* — slash any clothes — *(She makes a strange series of hand signs while moving her lips in unintelligible whispers. She reaches into her handbag. Rachel leaps back.)*

RACHEL: *Don't' shoot me* — *(Jill comes out of handbag with a handful of sparkling confetti. She flings it at Rachel. Rachel screams — leaps back — realizes it was confetti and settles down.)*

JILL: There — it's done.

RACHEL: You — messed up this floor.

JILL: The *floor?* Ha — I've messed up more than the floor — *(She chants.)*
I've messed up more
Than your pretty floor
Messed up more
Thank your chic little store
Messed you up more
Than you've been before.
(She laughs a strange cackling laugh.)

RACHEL: *I'm* responsible for this — *I'm* the one who'll have to sweep this stuff up.

JILL: This *stuff?* This *stuff* will do you in. I'm going to tell you something. I'm a witch. It's true — I'm a *witch.* I just put a curse on you — and this store. I did. I don't usually throw curses — I'm a good witch — I do *white* magic. But you pissed me off. You did. Now I'm sorry I did it — But it's done. I don't like losing control — we're supposed to keep our cool . . . Well — it's done.

RACHEL: And I have to sweep it up.

JILL: Stop worrying about sweeping it up. You have bigger things to worry about.

RACHEL: Really. *(She starts to sweep up confetti.)*

JILL: Yes, really . . . Really . . . You'd better . . . *do* something.

RACHEL: I'm *doing* something.

JILL: I mean *do* something.

RACHEL: What?

JILL: I don't know . . . Whatever people do — when they've been cursed. I can't — I'm usually at the other end of the cursing.

RACHEL: I think you got some of this stuff on the blouses.

JILL: Not that it would do much good. *Whatever* you did. It wouldn't take away the curse.

RACHEL: *You* are the curse. Coming in here — destroying this place just because you didn't know how to wash a blouse.

JILL: The curse *is* . . . Do you want to know what the curse is?

RACHEL: *Yes — please —* Tell me what the damn curse is and then get the hell out of here. *(She examines blouses, brushing confetti off them.)*

JILL: The *damn* curse — is not going to get the *hell* out of here. The *hell* will stay in . . . here — *(Pause.) Things* . . . will . . . fall *off.* That's it. Things will fall off.

RACHEL: Thank you. Now would you mind leaving?

JILL: Things will . . .

RACHEL: Fall off — I heard you. Would you leave? I'm going to call the police — *and — (She goes to phone.)* I'm going to call the owner — *(She opens notebook.)*

JILL: Monique.

RACHEL: Yes. And don't try to sneak a look at her number. *(She covers phone dial.)*

JILL: Tell her things will — *fall off. Blouses —* tell her blouses will — *fall —* off hangers — *Tags* will fall off blouses — *Sizes* will fall off collars — *Doors —* will fall — off — *hinges —* at — inopportune times — *Boxes* off *shelves — phones* off *desks —* and . . . *things* too late to be warned — be prepared — things will fall — *off* . . . first *buttons —* off *your* nonshrinking cotton blouse — *(She touches a button.)* The *name tag —* *(She touches it.)* the cotton *itself — (Touches.)* and

then . . . other things — *(Touches Rachel's breast.)* will fall — off —
(Rachel covers breast and steps back.)

RACHEL: Will *you* fall off — *get* off — get *out?*

JILL: Good-bye . . . I'm taking my blouse.

RACHEL: Take it. Go.

JILL: I'll give it to my sister. It may fit her five-year-old . . . Her name
is . . . Cindy . . . She's cute as a button — I'll tell my sister not to
wash it — just let the kid wear it till it disintegrates — with dirt —
(Goes to door.) Or — Or if she *does* wash it by mistake — Cindy can
give it to her dolly. . . . *(Almost out.)* Her name is *Pookie* . . . Cindy
and Pookie . . . *(She exits — Rachel stands looking after her. Rachel
looks down at confetti. Rachel looks at blouses. Rachel looks at phone.
The "All Cotton" sign falls off wall. Lights fade.)*

Any Place But Here
Caridad Svich

Dramatic

Lydia and Veronica (thirties)

> *Outside the factory on a lunch break. Lydia and Veronica, thirties, are seated on a small bench. Lydia is eating Cracker Jacks. Veronica is eating a sandwich. The women are longtime friends.*

VERONICA: I think I'm pregnant.

LYDIA: You killed a rabbit?

VERONICA: No, but I feel it. I feel something.

LYDIA: Could be indigestion.

VERONICA: Lydia!

LYDIA: You don't kill a rabbit, you don't know.

VERONICA: . . . I'm afraid.

LYDIA: Go see a doctor.

VERONICA: No.

LYDIA: Got to do something.

VERONICA: Got no insurance.

LYDIA: Go to the free clinic. I went.

VERONICA: You would.

LYDIA: Had to go somewhere.

VERONICA: That place is a slaughterhouse.

LYDIA: . . . You don't have to have it. . . . Have it, if that's what you want.

VERONICA: That's not what I want. Hell. I don't know what I want.

LYDIA: Look, kill a rabbit, then worry about it. You're gonna get a nervous breakdown like this.

VERONICA: Tommy's gonna kill me. If he finds out, he's gonna . . . he'll kill me.

LYDIA: Would you listen to yourself? You sound like me with Chucky: "He's gonna kill me, he's gonna kill me." Why's he gonna kill you? He don't want a kid?

VERONICA: It's not his.

LYDIA: What?

VERONICA: It's not.

LYDIA: . . . You didn't.

VERONICA: What do you expect me to do, wait around for Tommy til king-
dom come? He's at the fuckin bar all the time, when he comes home,
he couldn't see me from a bug on the wall he's so tired. I wait for
him to get it up . . .

LYDIA: He cares about you.

VERONICA: He don't know the first thing about me.

LYDIA: What are you talking about?

VERONICA: You think he knows what I want, what makes me feel good?
He don't know shit.

LYDIA: I always figured you was happy.

VERONICA: Happy?

LYDIA: . . . Whose is it?

VERONICA: I don't know.

LYDIA: You've been with more than one guy?

VERONICA: Yes.

LYDIA: . . . How many?

VERONICA: Not that many.

LYDIA: When are you gonna learn, huh? When are you gonna look at a
man's eyes for a change?

VERONICA: I wanna feel good. I like it. . . . Shit. Sometimes when I'm
fucking some guy, it's like . . . I'm happy, you know?

LYDIA: . . . You're in trouble. You're in serious trouble.

VERONICA: I know.

LYDIA: What are you going to do?

VERONICA: I ain't gonna have it. I ain't gonna have two babies suck me
dry. Not in my lifetime.

LYDIA: Two babies? Tommy ain't that bad.

VERONICA: You're gonna defend him now?

LYDIA: He ain't that bad. Hell. I wish Chucky were half as "bad" as Tommy.
Wouldn't mind it one bit.

VERONICA: . . . You got me all confused.

LYDIA: You were confused to start with. Now you're more confused. That's
the way it is.

VERONICA: I hate you.

> *(Pause. Lydia cries.)*

VERONICA: What?

LYDIA: Why do you do that?

VERONICA: What?

LYDIA: Why do you make me cry, huh? I got no one else to talk to, and you gotta make me cry. Don't look at me like that. You know what you said.

VERONICA: I ain't meant nothing.

LYDIA: "I hate you." What's that, huh? That don't mean nothing? Workin' fifteen hours a day, five, six days a week. Who am I gonna talk to, huh? . . . Look at me. I'm all wet. I can't stand it when I blubber.

VERONICA: I'm sorry.

LYDIA: And don't laugh. You always laugh when I cry. I hate that.

VERONICA: You got some snot on the side of your mouth.

LYDIA: Where?

VERONICA: On the side.

LYDIA: Here?

VERONICA: A little to the left.

LYDIA: Here?

VERONICA: Yeah.

LYDIA: *(Wipes if off with sleeve.)* Thanks.

> *(Pause.)*

VERONICA: What's up?

LYDIA: Huh?

VERONICA: What's with you?

LYDIA: Nothing.

VERONICA: Cryin' at the drop of a hat. Something's wrong. What is it?

LYDIA: . . . Chucky ain't touched me in weeks . . .

VERONICA: You talk to him?

LYDIA: Don't you listen to me? We don't talk no more. . . . I don't think he loves me. I don't think he does. No more.

> *(Pause.)*

VERONICA: Leave him. You could find out if you left him.

LYDIA: If he loves me?

VERONICA: Yes.

LYDIA: . . . I've thought about it. Then I think of him, what he'd do . . .
Don't feel right. Don't feel right. . . . I tried to kill myself. Thought about
it I don't know how many times . . . Never actually, you know . . . But
then the other day, he was sleeping so peaceful passed out, I thought
"I'm gonna do it. I'm gonna go out. For good." So I took his gun
and I . . . I was set, you know. I was set. I had the whole thing figured out. One shot . . . And then I thought "What am I doing? What
the fuck am I doing staring at a pink bedspread with a gun in my
hand trying to kill myself?" Seemed stupid. I felt so stupid . . . And
the thing I kept thinking of the most was the sound. If I pulled the
trigger, fired. How loud it would be. Sure to wake Chucky up. Wake
him up and then what? Just seemed stupid.

VERONICA: . . . Come 'ere.

LYDIA: Huh?

VERONICA: Come 'ere.

(Veronica holds her.)

VERONICA: Crazy girl. You're a fuckin' crazy girl. Gotta rest your mind.
Rest before it runs away from you. Thinking things like that?
Crazy. . . . Just think. What would I do without you? You think
about that? You put a gun against your head, you call me.

LYDIA: It was Saturday . . .

VERONICA: You call me. You don't do nothing. You call me. You hear what
I'm saying?

LYDIA: Yeah.

VERONICA: Swear to God. You scare me. The things you do, say . . .

LYDIA: I'm all right.

VERONICA: Yeah.

(Lydia nods. Beat.)

LYDIA: *(At end of Cracker Jacks box.)* Got a ring.

VERONICA: Put it on. Gift horse, ain't it?

LYDIA: *(Tries it.)* It don't fit.

*(The sound of a metallic horn — from the factory — is heard. Sound
stops.)*

VERONICA: Let's get back to work before they fire our ass.

(They exit. Lights fade.)

Autobiography of a Homegirl

Yvette Heyliger

Dramatic

Roanetta and Johnnie Mae (early thirties)

> Roanetta (early thirties) is a light-skinned African-American woman. Johnnie Mae (early thirties) is a dark-skinned African-American woman who is the godmother of Roanetta's daughter, Hope. The two women are neighbors and best friends.
>
> Set in 1983, this is a bittersweet play about Roanetta's epiphany when, in a twenty-four-hour stretch, her child's father shows up with his white fiancée; and in an historic coup, the first black woman is crowned Miss America.
>
> Scene: Roanetta's no-frills apartment in Harlem, N.Y.; Johnnie Mae has come to tell Roanetta the historic news that a black woman has won the Miss America pageant. This news opens up a can of worms, as these longtime friends learn for the first time that they have very different values and beliefs.
>
> Please note: This scene is a slightly revised version of the published one.

[HOPE: *(Still in a parental tone. Exiting.)* Now, don't let me have to come back out here!]

ROANETTA: See what you did? Keep your voice down.

JOHNNIE MAE: You keep your voice down. You started this field niggah business.

ROANETTA: Gee, I think you're taking this too personally.

JOHNNIE MAE: Damn right, it's personal. And I think you're going way off the deep end.

ROANETTA: Well, you started it. It's the same crap since junior high school.

Why is it that you have to be dark-skinned to be considered a real black person?

JOHNNIE MAE: Because that's the way it is. You always thought you were better than everybody else, anyway.

ROANETTA: I never said I was better than anybody! When did I ever say that? When?

JOHNNIE MAE: You didn't have to say anything. It was the way you talked, the way you dressed at school, the way you carried yourself — like you were better, privileged.

ROANETTA: Privileged? I can't help the way I was raised. I was in private schools up until the time I went to that school.

JOHNNIE MAE: Finally, here it comes, "the put-down." I knew it! I knew you thought you were better than everybody else because you were light-skinned.

ROANETTA: That's a lie! I changed the way I spoke, changed the way I dressed. But that wasn't enough. I didn't fit in at the white schools. I didn't fit in at the black schools. That didn't feel like being privileged to me. It just felt lonely.

JOHNNIE MAE: Oh, please! All the boys were interested in you, Roanetta.

ROANETTA: *(Surprised.)* Boys?! I wasn't interested in boys; I was interested in school!

JOHNNIE MAE: Yea, actin' all white.

ROANETTA: What is so wrong with being a good student? Why does that have to mean I was "acting white"? I busted my butt trying to fit in.

JOHNNIE MAE: Well, you fit in real good with the boys. They were interested in you, and all the other yellow girls with the "good hair." You've never been a little too black, with hair a little too kinky, nose a little too wide, lips a little too big, butt a little too broad, and feet a little too flat. Any boy that I wanted didn't want me; even my own mama didn't want me. See, I wasn't that pretty yellow baby she'd planned on, hoped for, had slept with that yellow man she ain't seen since, to get. When I was little I would get on my knees and pray, "Please Jesus, make me white." 'cause Mama always spoke so horribly about black people. "Look at those nappy-headed niggahs! Can't stand 'em. Can't stand niggahs." I couldn't' understand how she could say these things. I mean, didn't she know she was talking about me? She was talking about me! "But Mama," I'd say, "we're black." "Girl, no I'm not. I'm a white woman." You seen my mama, Roanetta! She's darker than me! My mama, black as me, talkin' bout she a white woman. When Mama give me a bath she would scrub me until it hurt — my black neck! She was scrubbing off my blackness. Don't deny it Ro, bein' light-skinned is your most precious possession!

ROANETTA: That is not true! Don't you know I would have traded, my hair, my skin color and my speech for one day of peace at that school! For one day of knowing what it felt like to be a "real black person," for one day of being a "homegirl." You don't know what it's like not to be accepted by your own people!

JOHNNIE MAE: Is that what this growing interest in Africa has been about — acceptance?

ROANETTA: Yes! I'm beginning to believe that the Motherland is the key, the solution to the differences between black people. We just have to practice remembrance. You see, we all come from the same place. Africa, which connects us on the *inside* no matter what our color is on the outside. We just have to wake up and remember we're all from the same place.

JOHNNIE MAE: You honestly think, looking like you do, that if you went over to the Motherland, they'd remember you? I don't think so, Ms. Tarzan.

ROANETTA: They will so! *(She gets the book of Africa proverbs. Reading.)* There is a Mandinka proverb that says:
nee mee ta dula long
tai ee bodola
eecee fung long
woto eecee ta dula long

JOHNNIE MAE: In English, please.

ROANETTA: "If you don't know where to go –" meaning, if you don't know who you are, Crystal; or what to do with your life, I guess. "Go back to where you come from — " meaning, you know your history. "And then you will know who you are really; and you will know where to go and — "

JOHNNIE MAE: Stop it! I can't go nowhere but where I am.

ROANETTA: You can!

JOHNNIE MAE: Y'all bourgeois folks don't know nothin' bout 'nowhere.'

ROANETTA: This proverb is about knowing where to go and what to do with our lives once we wake up an remember who we really are! African Kings and Queens, not slaves!

JOHNNIE MAE: Maybe you'd better wake up and "remember" that we are niggah's living in the Divided States of America; land of the free/home of the slave, where people like you think you're better than people like me. Admit it! You think you're better than me because you're light-skinned!

ROANETTA: No, Crystal, *you* think I'm better than you because I'm light-skinned! And I am sick to death of apologizing for who I am and how I look because of it. You know, I would like for once in my life, to feel comfortable in my own skin; to not be embarrassed by my own hair. I'm tired of feeling guilty because you're mad you don't look like me!

JOHNNIE MAE: What?!

ROANETTA: You're mad you don't look like me!

JOHNNIE MAE: I am not!

ROANETTA: Yes, you are.

JOHNNIE MAE: No, I'm not.

ROANETTA: Then why are you trying to change who you are: your name . . . the wigs?

JOHNNIE MAE: Why're you tryin' to change who you are? *(She does a mock African dance step, punctuating the syllables.)* Nee-mee-ta-doo-booga-boo!

ROANETTA: I'm embracing my past, *our past!*

(Roanetta does an authentic African dance step.)

JOHNNIE MAE: Well, I'm embracing my present, our present.

(Johnnie Mae does a 1980s dance step.)

ROANETTA: Well, like it or not, I am black too. And so is she. That light-skinned "sistah" is the first black woman to be crowned Miss America. She's making history, and all you can talk about is her light eyes, her light skin, a quarter of this and an eighth of that! Don't you take it away from her; don't you dare take it away from her.

JOHNNIE MAE: Why not? She's probably going to come out and say she's an "individual" and her being black has nothing to do with winning anyway. Why are you tryin' to act like you don't know what I'm talking about, Ro?

ROANETTA: I know exactly what you're talking about. You think because she's light-skinned, she's not worthy of winning, much less of being liked, respected, or even loved by her own people?

JOHNNIE MAE: I never said that.

ROANETTA: You didn't have to say it — this conversation says it all! My God, can't you see? Don't you even realize what she has done by winning that insipid, sexist pageant? For the first time, *we* are being publicly acknowledged as beautiful. Publicly! It's a coup d'etat!

JOHNNIE MAE: A coo-day-what?

ROANETTA: A coup d'etat — the sudden overthrow of a ruler. Don't you get it? *(She gets a chair from the kitchen/work table and places it in the middle of the room. It becomes "the pedestal" as Roanetta stands upon it.)* We're on the pedestal now! We're desirable, we're cherish-able; for once we as black women are prized above all others! Out of the kitchen and into the bedroom; this high yellow woman winning the Miss America title is a victory for all of us — for you and for me! We should be celebrating because somewhere, some little black girl is going to say to herself, I can achieve that. I can do that. I can become anything I want. She is inspired by her own self-esteem to accomplish great things. And I don't know about you, but I need a little inspiration right now. I need it. I feel so proud and I can't believe I'm saying it! Who knows, maybe they'll make the First Black Miss America Doll. Hey, this is perfect timing! I can include it in my article for *Essence. (Getting down, she goes to her desk to jot down her thoughts on a note pad.)* Our children need more black dolls to play with — black dolls that are positive reflections of themselves.

JOHNNIE MAE: *Yes, themselves.* Not you, and sure as hell not that Barbie doll Miss America! Don't you get it? It hurts me — and every other real black woman — just to look at you! *We* are not being publicly acknowledged as beautiful, *you* are! You always are!

ROANETTA: But, Johnnie Mae, that's not my fault! Come on. You know I always hated that stupid pageant, but you have to look at the larger picture.

JOHNNIE MAE: I am! You're the one up on the pedestal, not me. How's the air up there, huh?

(Johnnie Mae knocks over "the pedestal.")

ROANETTA: Wait a minute; this new Miss America is standing on the shoulders of you and me.

JOHNNIE MAE: *(Not buying it.)* Oh, please!

ROANETTA: Fine. Well then, maybe this will give you some comfort. No matter what the complexion of my skin, or how well I speak, or what class I am in, I'm still a nigger to a white person, aren't I? Aren't I? That's the bottom line, isn't it? Does that make you feel better?

JOHNNIE MAE: You just don't get it!

ROANETTA: All right! I admit it! I'm light-skinned. All right? I have good hair! My family is middle class! I admit it! Are you happy now? I'm guilty by birth, an event that, by the way, I had no control over. And you, and every other dark-skinned black person, are never going to let me forget it. Fine! But, let me ask you this — did I ever once put you down or make you feel less than? Was I ever unkind to you? Did I ever treat you the way Shaniqua and the rest of them treated me: escorting me home from school every day, threatening to beat me up because of the way I looked, no! But, I see now that you felt the same way they did. No wonder you never said anything in my defense.

JOHNNIE MAE: I wasn't going to get my ass kicked.

ROANETTA: Yet, you let me get mine kicked. And you're still kicking it, all of you! Look at how I am living my life. I'm struggling just like you are. Nothing's been handed to me. I'm trying to find my place in the world on my own terms just like you are. I'm not living some uppity lifestyle on the East Side or some place. I'm here in Harlem just like you are!

JOHNNIE MAE: That is your choice. You don't have to be here. I do. I belong here in the dark, dirty fields of Harlem! *(She exits leaving the door open.)*

(Roanetta gently picks up "the pedestal." Setting the chair upright, she places it back at the kitchen table.)

(Johnnie Mae returns.) And I'll tell you somethin' else; any black man

that wants you really wants a white woman anyway. But, if Craig had gotten a taste of a *real* black woman, instead of a wanna-be, he never would have gone over to the other side! Now, put that in your little article for *Essence* magazine and smoke it!

(Johnnie Mae exits.)

Beautiful Clear-Eyed Woman

Diana Amsterdam

Dramatic

Theodora and Franny (forties)

> Theodora Woolsey, forty-eight, has come unexpectedly to visit Franny
> Woolsey, forty-one, her old friend and ex-sister-in-law. Theodora is
> divorced from Frank, Franny's brother — the rich one in the fam-
> ily. Until recently, the elderly father has been in Franny's care; but
> Theodora has been carefree pursuing her successful career in Dublin.
> But now the old man has died, Theodora's daughter has gone miss-
> ing and Theodora comes back.

THEODORA: I hear you may be getting married again.

FRANNY: You really have heard just about . . .

FRANNY: . . . every goddamn thing   THEODORA: I hear he's a
there is to hear.   pediatrician — how perfect!

THEODORA: . . . and a widower — how divine!

FRANNY: OK. Y'know what? You want to be talking to your daughter, not
me . . .

FRANNY: . . . about this.   THEODORA: No. I want to be . . .

THEODORA: . . . talking to you. I want to be talking to you. Do you know
that I've felt guilty about you for twenty-five years . . .

FRANNY: Oh come on.   THEODORA: Yes, I have — you
What?   the poor relation . . .

THEODORA: . . . you the single mother, you the caregiver — and then I
hear that Po has died, and I'm thinking: Finally, this must be amazing for Franny, she's finally free! and I'm thinking, I'm must thinking, how I'm going to give you a nice chunk of money . . .

FRANNY: You are?   THEODORA: . . . part of the
absurdly huge . . .

THEODORA: . . . settlement I got from Frank — yup — when I hear you may be getting married again! You're just free, and you may be getting married!

FRANNY: Yes — that's true.

THEODORA: Don't do it, Franny. I am saying to you, not my daughter, but to you: Don't. If you get married, you'll never see your, your life's work.

FRANNY: Oh, that's, that's just — old, I can be married and also do my work. If you want to tell your daughter something, tell her she can have a relationship and also do anything she wants, she can, if she's with the right person . . .

FRANNY: . . . and David — that's   THEODORA: Ah:
his name . . .   the right person.

FRANNY: . . . David — but then I'm sure you know that — David is the right person.

THEODORA: Has he had children?

FRANNY: No.

THEODORA: Is he going to want children?

FRANNY: I don't know — he might, want, a child or two . . .

FRANNY: . . . but I'm just going to   THEODORA: But of course you're
have one — I've already   thinking of it — just one!
made up my mind to that
much — I'm just gonna have   — the word "just"
one child with him.   does not apply to children . . .

THEODORA: Franny, you're just gonna have one child? Don't you remember what it's like? It takes up your entire life . . .

FRANNY: OK, y'know what?   THEODORA: . . . you've got this thing
I don't really want to be   on you all the time, Jesus,
talking about this right   you'll be writing on the toilet,
now — I don't want to be   if you can get to the toilet —
talking about this!   What is causing . . .

THEODORA: . . . this amnesia? Did something hit you on the head? Or is it the sex?

(Franny reacts.)

What is making you forget everything you know?

FRANNY: I haven't forgotten anything. I can just — see — something new.

I can see David. How good he is. And that he loves me, and I love him.

THEODORA: He loves you, you love him — can I have one of your smokes, please, are they filtered? Whatever — thanks — When Lisa says that? I'll be hard put to reply because she's seventeen and doesn't know shit — but when you say it, I can remind you of something you do know, love may fade but housework is forever.

FRANNY: Housework?

THEODORA: Yes, housework.

FRANNY: We're not talking about housework.

THEODORA: Children are housework, elderly parents are housework, husbands are housework, houses are housework . . .

FRANNY: David would do just as much of the housework as me. David would do just as much. Will you shut up and let me finish, you are exactly exactly like Frank sometimes!	THEODORA: . . . every single thing in most women's lives — every person I should say — represents an additional load of housework — the thing that kills us — housework —

THEODORA: OK I'll be quiet. Go on.

FRANNY: David is — well, he's exceptional. He cooks — he actually cooks — OK make a face but he does, and he cleans, he shops — he's a fully vested human being, he works right alongside me, and he notices he notices what I'm doing and how I'm feeling, as much as I notice him. David would never let me be crushed by housework, ever again, David loves me too much for that.

THEODORA: And what would he do with this? *(Holds up a coffee cup.)*

FRANNY: That?

THEODORA: When I am finished with my cup, you know, you don't even have to think, I'll take it to the sink, I'll take it I'll wash it I might even dry it, but a man? He will leave his cup on the table, unless you remind him to take it and then he'll say something like *(Indignantly:)* "I'm going to take it," and then he still doesn't take it, he starts reading the paper and you go through an inner debate about whether to mention it again because you might make him angry, so you go and throw another load of laundry in and when you come out? The damn coffee cup is still on the table and the man is nowhere to be seen and you pick the thing up and think how you should've done it yourself in the first place! You gave twenty years of your life to taking care of people's coffee cups, to the picking up, the washing up, the shopping and the cooking, do you need to enter into that again? Now is the time for you. Now is the time to fill your mind with things that are bigger than this *(The cup.)* see how it feels, see what kind of power you can find.

Bee-Luther-Hatchee
Thomas Gibbons

Dramatic

Shelita (midthirties, African-American); Anna (midthirties, white)

Shelita and Anna are celebrating Shelita's recent success as the editor of a best-selling memoir.

A bar. Anna sits at a table sipping a drink. She is white, in her midthirties, well-dressed. A martini is placed in front of the second chair. After a moment Shelita hurries on.

SHELITA: Anna — sorry I'm late. The traffic — !

ANNA: I was afraid you didn't have time for me anymore, what with picking up awards and being interviewed by the *Times.*

SHELITA: Until the story comes out you're still my friend. After that . . .
(They laugh. Shelita sits and sees the drink.)
Is this mine?

ANNA: I ordered for you.

SHELITA: Thanks.
(She takes a sip.)

ANNA: So when does the story come out?

SHELITA: Next week sometime — he wasn't sure. *(Pause.)* It was so *strange,* Anna. You think you're prepared, you're going to get your points across, and suddenly it veers off in a completely unexpected direction . . .

ANNA: Never trust a journalist. Especially not a good one. He didn't get you to say anything embarrassing, did he?

SHELITA: No.
(Suddenly she takes a deep breath.)

ANNA: Are you OK?

SHELITA: I just have to catch my breath. I feel like I can't *breathe.* Things are . . . eventful right now.

ANNA: You have a book on the best-seller list. Enjoy it!

SHELITA: There's something else.

ANNA: Really? *(She smiles.)* Have you met someone?

SHELITA: No, it's the same old desert out there.

(She grins, enjoying the suspense.)

I've been offered a job — by one of the big houses. I can't tell you which one, it might jinx it.

ANNA: It's not us, is it?

SHELITA: No. They took me out to lunch today and dropped it on me. Senior editor. More money — a lot more! — a corner office, A-list authors . . . or at least the top of the B list.

ANNA: Shelita, this is wonderful. You're a *star*. Let's order champagne!

(She turns to signal a waiter.)

SHELITA: No, please, Anna . . . Nothing is definite.

ANNA: Why not? You're taking it, aren't you?

SHELITA: I told them I needed to think about it.

ANNA: What's to think about?

SHELITA: It's not so simple. I'd have to walk away from what I'm doing now — and what I'm doing is important. And it's *mine* — my own series.

ANNA: For a small house that's . . .

SHELITA: "Marginal"?

ANNA: I was going to say "specialized." Come on, Shelita: Transit has a hard time getting its books in the stores, much less getting reviews, *attention* . . .

SHELITA: We're getting attention now.

ANNA: *Be-luther-hatchee* has put you at the center of things — for a moment. Take advantage of it.

SHELITA: I don't know, Anna, a house like this, it's so . . .

ANNA: "White"?

SHELITA: I was going to say "mainstream."

ANNA: Do they publish any black writers?

SHELITA: A few. They'd like to find more. The black voice is hot right now.

ANNA: So they came to you.

SHELITA: It's just about making money to them, that's all.

ANNA: Well, of *course*.

SHELITA: It's about something else to me. *(Pause.)* I have to admit, though . . . working on Libby's book has made me a little impatient with the past. I want the new. The manuscript no one's read before.

ANNA: They're giving you the chance, Shelita. While they're making money, you can find the next Libby Price. A twenty-five-year-old Libby Price with a lifetime of books to write. And if you do it in a bigger office with a nicer view, what's wrong with that?

(A pause, then Shelita smiles.)

SHELITA: Trees outside my window . . . That would be nice.

(At once Anna motions offstage.)

ANNA: Waiter — a bottle of your best champagne! *(She turns to Shelita with a smile.)* I've always wanted to say that.

(They laugh.)

Bee-Luther-Hatchee
Thomas Gibbons

Dramatic

Shelita (midthirties, African-American); Anna (midthirties, white)

> Shelita reveals to Anna that Libby Price, the author of a best-selling
> memoir Shelita has edited, did not live at the nursing home she gave
> as her address. Furthermore, Shelita has lied to a reporter about ever
> actually meeting her.

*A restaurant. Shelita and Anna are having dinner. A folded section of
the* New York Times *lies on the table.*

SHELITA: It's outrageous. It's despicable.

ANNA: Why?

SHELITA: What he chose to include. How he presented me.

ANNA: It's a good story. You should be thrilled.

SHELITA: Anna, don't you *see?*

ANNA: No.

SHELITA: What it implies about me. *(She picks up the paper and reads:)*
" 'I want to say to her, as a young woman of color to her elder, as a
daughter, that her life has given me an example of courage and dignity — 'At this point Ms. Burns' eyes clouded over, and she was unable to finish her thought."
(She slaps the paper down.)

ANNA: And that implies — well, what? That you're human, you have emotions? Yes, that is outrageous.
(She smiles, but Shelita refuses to be deflected from her anger.)

SHELITA: Anna, it says that I'm weak and incompetent.

ANNA: It says that you care about the books you publish. What's wrong
with that?

SHELITA: "Her eyes clouded over, she was unable to finish her thought — "
Don't you recognize the *code?*

ANNA: I recognize the code when I see it. This is not the code.

SHELITA: He could have said, "She left her phrase unfinished" or any one of a dozen other things. But he chose a particular combination of words to convey the impression that I'm overly emotional and not quite capable.

ANNA: Why would he do that?

SHELITA: Because he hasn't been given his own column. Because he has the Great American Novel in his desk drawer and can't get it published. Because I'm a black woman, I'm successful, and I have to be put in my place. Pick one.

ANNA: *(Picks up the paper:)* You really believe he did it deliberately?

SHELITA: Well, if he did it unconsciously, it's even worse, isn't it? *(Pause.)* A white person writes about a black person, and those condescending words creep in. Or else it's that bending-over-backwards, look-everyone-*I'm-* not-a-racist tone. You can always tell.

ANNA: *(Noncommittal:)* Hmm. *(She studies the article.)* The picture is good, though.

(Pause.)

SHELITA: Not bad. *(They laugh, Shelita a bit ruefully.)* I'm sorry, Anna, it's just . . . Something very strange happened a couple of days ago. You know I went to Charlotte to meet Libby. At the nursing home.

ANNA: Yes.

(Shelita says nothing.)

And — ?

SHELITA: She wasn't there.

ANNA: She moved?

SHELITA: She never lived there. They had no idea who Libby Price was.

ANNA: *(Frowning.)* That's odd . . .

SHELITA: Then I remembered her royalties go to a lawyer in Charlotte. When I called him, he said he couldn't tell me her address. "My client's wishes."

ANNA: But wait — what about the story? *(She picks up the paper.)* Right here. "About her long-anticipated meeting with — "

SHELITA: *(Quoting from memory:)* " — with her reclusive author, Ms. Burns was circumspect. 'It went fine,' she said, and volunteered nothing further. Apparently Libby Price is to remain, at least to everyone else, a tantalizing mystery."

ANNA: But why did he — *(Pause.)* He invented this?

SHELITA: Not exactly . . . He called back the next day and asked about our meeting.

ANNA: And you told him it went fine? Why on earth did you say that?

SHELITA: I don't know . . . He caught me off guard. The words just slipped out.

ANNA: *(In a still voice:)* My God — you lied. *(Suddenly she bursts into laughter.)* You *lied*. To a *journalist*. From the *Times*.

SHELITA: I didn't mean —

ANNA: I'm so proud of you!

SHELITA: Anna —

ANNA: And now you're afraid he'll find out, right? That he'll turn the blinding spotlight of his moral outrage on you? Journalists are lied to all the time, Shelita. They expect it — they *crave* it. After all, if people simply told them the truth, what fun would they have?

SHELITA: I don't care about *him,* Anna. Why did Libby lie to *me*?

ANNA: For the same reason anyone does. She has something to protect. *(She gestures dismissively.)* She's an old woman, Shelita. Allow her a few eccentricities.

SHELITA: I've checked with friends at other houses. *Bee-luther-hatchee* didn't make the usual rounds. Libby sent it to *me*. I worked on it for a year. You know what it's like — you write back and forth, you share things. I even told her about Paul.

ANNA: That *jerk. (She shakes her head.)* Men with rings . . .

SHELITA: Libby and I have a relationship.

ANNA: You're her editor, that's all. Don't confuse it with something else.

SHELITA: Like what?

ANNA: Come on, Shelita, it must have occurred to you before now. It's so *obvious. (She reads from the article:)* "I want to say to her as a young woman of color to her elder, as a *daughter* — "

SHELITA: What are you — I didn't mean it *literally.*

ANNA: It's the word you used.

SHELITA: *(Angrily:)* This is ridiculous. Libby is not some kind of mother substitute.

ANNA: As long as I've known you — what is it, ten, *twelve* years now? —

the subject of your family has been off limits. You never talk about them.

SHELITA: That's not true — I have told you. My father died, my mother left. I was raised by my grandmother. Until I was twelve years old I thought *she* was my mother.

ANNA: A few facts, yes. Then the wall goes up. It's going up *now.*

SHELITA: I don't believe in advertising my pain, Anna.

ANNA: You don't believe in opening up. My parents' breakup was painful for me, and you've heard every last detail. *(Pause.)* Do you remember your mother at all?

(Pause.)

SHELITA: I have a vague memory of someone. *(Her tone is exasperated, but as she continues she is drawn into the memory.)* I was playing in the living room one day — I must have been four or five. My grandmother was upstairs cleaning. And a woman appeared at the screen door. . . .

Then my grandmother came down the steps and told me to go to my room. Her voice was quiet but I could see she was upset. Sitting on my bed, I could hear their voices floating up through the floor. Angry words. The door slammed. When I looked out my window I saw the woman walking down the street, fast. I remember staring at her and thinking, turn around, look back. Look at me. I wanted to see her face. But she turned the corner and disappeared.

(After a moment Anna murmurs sympathetically:)

ANNA: Shelita, I'm so . . .

SHELITA: Was it even her? It was a long time ago.

ANNA: Did you ever try to find her?

SHELITA: It's not like an adoption. When people vanish, they don't leave records. *(Pause.)* I hired a private detective about ten years ago. He felt sorry for me, I think — I certainly couldn't afford to pay him much. He never came up with anything, though. *(A moment, then she shrugs.)* So — a story without an ending. And it has nothing to do with Libby.

ANNA: If you say so.

SHELITA: Her book has changed my life, Anna. And she's *alive.* Is it so strange that I want to meet her?

ANNA: Writers create illusions out of the best part of themselves. What's
     left over can be . . .

SHELITA: What?

ANNA: A disappointing reality. Leave her alone.

SHELITA: For all I know, she's working on another book. If she is, I want
     to sign it. Imagine walking into the new job with *that* contract in
     my pocket!

ANNA: So how are you going to find your reclusive author?

SHELITA: I wrote her a letter about my trip to the nursing home. Asking
     why she found it necessary to deceive me. *(Pause.)* I wasn't very nice.

ANNA: Any answer?

SHELITA: Not yet.

ANNA: *(Sighing:)* I envy you, Shelita.

SHELITA: Me? Why?

ANNA: Look at us. Two attractive, reasonably successful women — *very*
     successful, in your case — and what are we doing? Having yet an-
     other dinner together. At least *you* have a mystery to solve.

SHELITA: Just call me a Nancy Drew for the new millennium.

ANNA: *(Picking up the paper:)* The *Times* will probably do another story
     when you *do* find her.

     (Shelita takes a drink. Anna's eye is caught by something.)

     Hmm . . .

SHELITA: What?

ANNA: This last sentence: "Apparently Libby Price is to remain, *at least to
     everyone else,* a tantalizing mystery."

SHELITA: What about it?

ANNA: Well, it didn't occur to me before. But if you read it in a certain
     way . . . *(She looks up at Shelita.)* He almost seems to be suggesting
     that *you* wrote the book.

Cairo
Arthur Melville Pearson

Dramatic

Jane and Jan (twenties to thirties)

> Near the top of the play in a converted chicken coop in Cairo (pro-
> nounced KAY-ro), Illinois. Jane Jennsen — a university administra-
> tor in her late twenties/early thirties and the only sibling to "escape"
> the family farm — has just returned to deal with her brother's lat-
> est schizophrenic crisis spurred by the impending sale of the family
> farm. Jan is the middle daughter who stayed and self-appointed care-
> taker to everyone but herself. The two sisters love each other deeply,
> which means they know exactly how to push each other's buttons
> to maximum value.

Jane holds out a letter.

JANE: What's this?

JAN: What?

JANE: This.

JAN: What?! Oh, you didn't get one?

JANE: What *is* this?

JAN: Why's he only send me this crap? You're gonna love this, read it.

JANE: From James?

JAN: Chock full o' nuts.

JANE: This looks like a . . . what, a . . . my God!

JAN: Mm-hm.

JANE: When did you receive this? It's dated a week ago, why didn't you
    tell me about this?

JAN: It's no different from the other ones he sends me.

JANE: Jan!

JAN: It slipped my mind.

JANE: Your brother's request for funeral arrangements?

JAN: Anyone with half a brain can see it doesn't make sense, anyway.

JANE: It makes sense to James.

JAN: And no one else — buried with books — are you going to make that coffee or what? I'll make it. *(Jan takes over the coffee duties while Jane is immersed in the letter.)* So, what time do you think we should expect Mama?

JANE: Jan.

JAN: Will she have to be back before the dawn?

JANE: Jan!

JAN: "Jan," "Jan," you sound like a broken record or something, what time should we expect Mama?

JANE: I'm trying to read.

JAN: I mean, it's been quite some time, I wonder what she looks like?

JANE: If you don't want to be here you don't have to, you know, I just thought you might be a bit concerned, that you'd want to be here.

JAN: Wait a minute, I'm here all the time, I live here, remember?

JANE: I know.

JAN: I'm not the one who lives three hours away should something really happen.

JANE: I know.

JAN: And I am concerned, but I refuse to mope around like she really is going to show up or something.

JANE: Who's to say?

JAN: Oh, now stop, stop, right at the stroke of midnight, Mama's gonna pull up in a blue car with Grammie and Grampa and take James away with them.

JANE: A blue '51 Chevy, I told you.

JAN: Whatever!

JANE: What I am saying is that James believes it.

JAN: But it's not true!

JANE: Whether it's true or not to us is not the point.

JAN: No, the point is the family squirrel says jump and all us nuts say, "How high?"

JANE: I wish to heaven you had told me about this sooner, did you even read this?

JAN: Janey. Listen to me. It is no different from the letters I get from him all the time.

JANE: Funeral arrangements? Christ, Jan.

JAN: Jesus wasn't an Egyptian.

JANE: Excuse me?

JAN: Jesus wasn't an Egyptian. Mm-hm, he sends me this one letter tells me he can't go to church anymore because the bible is just a plagiarized version of the Book of the Dead.

JANE: What, the Egyptian Book of the Dead?

JAN: No, the Cleveland Book of the Dead.

JANE: There's the Tibetan one, too, smartie, but what does he say about the Bible?

JAN: I don't know, he rattles on about all these parallels — death and rebirth, judgment in the afterlife and . . . oh, and this one passage when an Egyptian god is called "King of Kings," you know word for word just like in the Christmas thing, you know . . . *(Half-singing, trying to remember:)* "King of Kings and Lord of Lords."

JANE: The *Messiah?* The *Hallelujah Chorus?* That's in the Book of the Dead?

JAN: I guess, less the music I suppose, why's he only send me this crap?

JANE: You're his twin.

JAN: *(Vehemently:)* Through no fault of mine! He never sends this crap to you?

JANE: Tell me if this makes any sense to you . . . his letter says he wants to be buried with the Book of The Complete Poems of Carl Sandburg, the Book of Vachel Lindsay Collected Poems . . . see? The book of, the book of, the real titles of these books don't start with the book of.

JAN: "The Book of" the Dead.

JANE: Exactly.

JAN: So he gets the titles confused.

JANE: And what is the Book of the Dead used for?

JAN: How to make a mummy.

JANE: It's a road map for what happens after you die. Here, take this and read the books he's listed.

(Jan reads the letter to herself.)

Out loud.

JAN: What are you doing?

JANE: Seeing if the books he's listed are here, they might tell us something.

JAN: This is creepy.

JANE: Keep reading. Out loud.

JAN: The Book of Spoon River Anthology.

JANE: *(Finding it:)* Yes!

JAN: First volume?

JANE: No, second.

JAN: His letter says, "Volume I, Not Volume II."

JANE: Let me see. *(Taking the letter.)* And "Not Volume II" is double-underlined. Shoot.
(Jan picks up Volume II, opens the front cover and screams.)
What?!

JAN: Get it away, Jane, get it away!

JANE: What?!

JAN: It's still alive!

JANE: *(Grabbing the book and reading:)* "James Jennsen, Cairo High, Declamatory Speech . . ."

JAN & JANE: Mrs. Z!!!

JAN: *(From memory, as if Pavlov rang a bell:)* Out of me unworthy and unknown/The vibrations of deathless music/'With malice toward none, with charity for all'/Out of me the forgiveness of millions toward millions.

JANE: Brava!

JAN: Old bat beat it into my head.

JANE: You could always remember pieces better than I could, almost better than Mama could.

JAN: Yeah, but you could recite them better, who did you do?

JANE: The one Master wrote about his own grandmother, always reminded me of Mama, her spirit anyway.

JAN: Lucinda Matlock.

JANE: You're memory's not so bad after all.

JAN: Well, with Mrs. Z riding roughshod.

JANE: Final project?

JAN: A selection from one of the Illinois poets.

JANE: Sandburg.

JAN: Lindsay.

JANE: Masters, or . . . ?

JAN: Gettysburg Address.

JANE: Extra credit for one poem and the address?

(The gauntlet is down.)

JAN & JANE: Four score and seven years ago, our fathers brought forth upon this continent a new nation, conceived in liberty and dedicated to the proposition that 'all men are created equal.'

JAN: You don't remember the whole thing, do you?

JANE: Don't you?

JAN: Brain.

JANE: Twerp.

JAN: Nerd.

JANE: Runt.

JAN: Hate you.

JANE: Hate you back.

JAN: Last word, jinx.

JANE: Fingers crossed, last word, jinx. *(The two sisters share a much-needed laugh.)* Miss me?

JAN: Maybe. You?

JANE: Very much. *(This is the first relaxed moment between them.)* How are you? *(A look from Jan.)* No, *really.*

JAN: Sit down, you haven't stopped moving since you got here.

(Jane finally sits.)

JANE: It's good to see you.

JAN: How are things in the ivory tower?

JANE: That's ivy, if you please.

JAN: Tomayta, Tomahta, the big U.

JANE: Crazy, sure, but things are exciting, enrollment is up for the third year in a row, a lot more women are attending . . . *(No response from Jan.)* And the twins?

JAN: Weeds, like weeds, I can't keep 'em in pants, by the way, thanks for the Power Rangers jammies, they love them, they adore you, I don't buy them that crap.

JANE: You're welcome. Don?

JAN: Drunk, want that warmed?

(Jan pours another round.)

JANE: Thank you. Those meetings didn't help?

JAN: Nope, they put him on that drug, whatever it is, makes you sick if you so much as think about taking a drink. All that meant I was cleaning up what his guts couldn't keep down, I can take him drunk, it's neater.

JANE: Did you find anything else with the PJs I sent?

JAN: I don't know, Jane, did I find anything else with the PJs you sent?

JANE: Application forms, information about correspondence courses?

JAN: Still out to run the world.

JANE: No.

JAN: Yes, and yes, I found the information and yes, I appreciate the sisterly nudge.

JANE: I don't mean to stick my nose in where it doesn't . . .

JAN: So don't.

JANE: You probably promised yourself you'd pursue a degree once you . . .

JAN: Well, with two sprouts and a sot, I've just about got my hands full.

JANE: The longer you wait, the harder . . .

JAN: The harder it'll be for you to start your family.

(Buttons have been pushed as only close sisters can — Jane is up on her feet.)

JANE: Look, I didn't come all the way down here for this.

JAN: Just what did you come down here for?

JANE: James needs help.

JAN: Not the kind you can give him, sister, I'm here to tell you this is one thing you can't fix.

JANE: I can start by giving him the attention and care he deserves.

JAN: Listen to yourself, you sound like a textbook or somethin', we take care of James just fine without you.

JANE: Obviously not or he wouldn't be requesting his funeral arrangements.

JAN: I do his dirty laundry once a week.

JANE: I know.

JAN: I bring the squirrel hot meals three times a week.

JANE: I know.

JAN: I'm not the one who visits the fruitcake only on Christmas!

JANE: Well a Christian martyr you are, Jan, a Christian martyr. *(Jane stretches her arms out like the crucifixion.)* Hey, can you see my house from up there?

JAN: Listen, you left.

JANE: And you stayed.

JAN: And I married.

JANE: And you had to.

JAN: For the last time, that is not true!

JANE: It is true.

JAN: Someone wanted me.

JANE: Yes, barefoot, dumb, and pregnant.

JAN: Well, speaking of pregnant . . .

JANE: Stop right there.

Gorgeous Raptors
Lucy Alibar-Harrison

Seriocomic

Kaballah and Elise (both sixteen)

> Kaballah and Elise are both sixteen and becoming best friends. They
> escape their less-than-attractive lives by pretending to be powerful,
> beautiful raptors. Here, Kaballah reveals a dark secret from her past.

*Lights up on Kaballah and Elise after several hours of drinking from an
open bottle of wine and several bottles of beer. Inebriation has been a
catalyst for their camaraderie; they are laughing loudly and feeding each
other marshmallows as they cling to each other.*

KABALLAH: They're monsters! When I graduate I'm gonna move to San
Francisco and become a lesbian.

ELISE: You can't let a couple of jerks represent a whole gender.

KABALLAH: It's not just that. I see a guy, I imagine him naked and I just
want to laugh.

ELISE: Laugh?

KABALLAH: You'd understand if you'd seen one naked.

ELISE: I've seen them naked. I've done more stuff than you. I like how
they look naked.

KABALLAH: Oh, I don't. Ugh.

ELISE: Kaballah? Have you ever thought — I don't know. Have you ever
thought you might actually be a lesbian?

KABALLAH: I don't want to talk about that.

ELISE: Alright. I'm sorry, I talk a lot and I don't know when to shut up.
Which is now.

KABALLAH: Maybe. Yes. No. I'm not. If I'm going to be a lesbian, I want
it to be because I'm attracted to women. And I don't think I am. I
just hate men.
(They both collapse into drunken laughter.)

KABALLAH: Seriously, though. They always seem like they're ready to pounce. Like all intellect and morality is abandoned as soon as they see breasts.

(Elise hugs her, which she concedes to after a beat. Kaballah finally nestles with her head in Elise's lap.)

ELISE: When you did that thing to your wrists — were you trying to kill yourself?

KABALLAH: Nope. Who's the strangest guy you've ever wanted to schwamp?

ELISE: I used to want to fuck Mr. Clean's brains out.

KABALLAH: Mr. Clean? The guy with the tile cleaner?

ELISE: Wanted to fuck his brains out. Oh, God, did I say "fuck"?

KABALLAH: You wanted to schwamp MR. CLEAN?

ELISE: Don't laugh. He was sexy.

KABALLAH: I always thought Mr. Clean was gay.

ELISE: I hate you.

KABALLAH: He was so gay! He wore those tight little T-shirts that let you see his nipples? He was like the gay best friend of all the fifties housewives.

ELISE: I'm not hearing this!

KABALLAH: I think he and the Jolly Green Giant were a thing, actually.

ELISE: Kaballah, stop it! My childhood is being like, diaplated!

KABALLAH: Dilapidated.

ELISE: I can't believe I told someone that. Is there anymore beer?

KABALLAH: I don't think I can move to check.

ELISE: You barely drank anything. Which means I did . . .

KABALLAH: Let's just lie here. I like being petted. Awwwwk.

ELISE: You're nutty.

KABALLAH: Awwwk?

(She bats at Elise with her paws.)

ELISE: Don't make fun of me.

KABALLAH: I'm not making fun of you. Awwwwk.

(A giggly raptor fight ensues, ending in hysterical laughter.)

KABALLAH: I'm not a virgin!

ELISE: Ha! I knew it! I knew you weren't!

KABALLAH: Well, I'm not.

ELISE: I knew it I knew it I knew it! You have to tell me everything, Kaballah.

KABALLAH: I was four and one of my preschool teachers took me into the lost and found during lunchtime and gave me a Twizzler and took my clothes off and things got cuh-ray-zeee!

Is there anymore beer?

It's not like it sounds. It wasn't . . . I wouldn't call it rape or anything. I didn't do anything to make him stop.

ELISE: What does that mean?

KABALLAH: I didn't do anything to make him stop. If I had asked him to stop I'm sure he would have stopped. It doesn't matter. Forget I said anything.

ELISE: Did you tell your parents?

KABALLAH: You've met my parents. Do you think they'd be able to handle that?

ELISE: I don't know what to say.

KABALLAH: Don't say anything. I don't know why I told you that. I talk too much.

ELISE: I hate men, too. Why can't we do like your dad said? About taking to the streets and fighting?

KABALLAH: We don't want to get our hair messed up.

ELISE: No! Listen to me, Kaballah! They fought back. Why can't we?

KABALLAH: What is there to fight against? You can't just go and beat up all the monsters out there. Most of them work out.

ELISE: No, not the people. It's not the people. It's a thing. It's a Plague.

KABALLAH: A Plague? I never thought of it like that. I just figured men are jerks. Better to be a lesbian.

ELISE: Being a lesbian just because you don't want to deal with jerks is just another way of surrendering. It's a Plague, Kaballah! It attacks everyone. And it makes some girls really pretty by hollowing them out. And it turns some men into monsters. And they go out and they — they hurt people. Like they hurt you. Maybe that's why we're Raptors. We haven't been stricken with the Plague.

KABALLAH: I'll protect you, Elise.

ELISE: I'll protect you. At least from the Plague. You better not hack up your wrists anymore.

KABALLAH: To Raptors. May we never know Pretty.

Gorgeous Raptors
Lucy Alibar-Harrison

Seriocomic

Kaballah and Elise (both sixteen)

> Kaballah is the Weird Girl and Elise, the Shy Girl. Here, Elise's friend
> Justin has just forced a kiss on Kaballah, who fled in disgust and
> shame. Kaballah invites Elise into her fantasy Dinosaur world.

Kaballah spreads her arms, revealing gashes on the wrists that look a few
days old. Elise involuntarily gasps and Kaballah whirls around.

KABALLAH: Fuck you, bitch.

ELISE: That's ugly.

KABALLAH: Don't fucking moralize to me, you bitch.

ELISE: You're right, you have every right to say whatever you want to me.

KABALLAH: I don't want to say anything to you.

  I think homosexuality is genetic about 90 percent of the time.
  I think the other 10 percent are women that don't want to deal with
  troglodytes like them.

ELISE: What's a troglodyte?

KABALLAH: Why don't you look it up in the dictionary on your way to
  hell?

ELISE: I'm sorry, Kaballah. I didn't know he was going to do that.

KABALLAH: Bullshit you didn't know.

ELISE: Please don't say that! Please. It really offends me.

KABALLAH: You're pretty fucking entitled, aren't you?

  All right. I'm not going to apologize, but all right.

ELISE: Thank you. I didn't know Justin was going to kiss you.

KABALLAH: He didn't kiss me. He rammed his tongue down my throat
  while you sat there and laughed.

ELISE: What was I supposed to do, Kaballah?

KABALLAH: You could have said something. You could have told him to
  stop.

ELISE: I can't do that.

KABALLAH: You can't say "Stop?"

ELISE: I can't be mean.

KABALLAH: Letting him do that wasn't mean?

ELISE: I can't give people orders.

KABALLAH: You ordered me not to say "Fuck."

ELISE: I can't do that to boys. You don't need to look at me like that.

KABALLAH: I'm sorry, that just strikes me as very weird.

ELISE: Don't talk to me about weird, Raptor Girl.

KABALLAH: Why the hell do you do that?

ELISE: Please!

KABALLAH: Are you some kind of misogynist?

ELISE: I don't know. I don't even know what that word means.

KABALLAH: I mean, do you feel an overwhelming hatred for all women, including yourself, because there is nothing redeeming about you save your sexual allure to men?

ELISE: Why do you always wear those big jackets? And those hats?

KABALLAH: I'm cold.

ELISE: It's eighty-eight degrees!

KABALLAH: Those are numbers. I'm cold.

ELISE: Stop lying, Kaballah. You don't have to tell me why you dress like that, but don't lie.

KABALLAH: I'm not lying. I feel cold.

ELISE: I saw your wrists.

KABALLAH: I'm thrilled beyond belief. Please go away.

ELISE: Did you do that to yourself?

KABALLAH: I'm a prophet. I received the stigmata.

ELISE: On your arms and wrists?

KABALLAH: He missed. God pointed down from the sky and was like, "I give you stigmata! Bam!" but he'd been drinking.

ELISE: Were you trying to kill yourself?

KABALLAH: My cat scratched me.

ELISE: Does your cat smoke crack?

KABALLAH: Why are you talking to me?

ELISE: I want you to understand things, Kaballah.

KABALLAH: I understand that you're much crazier than I am, even if you don't want to think so.

ELISE: I'm sorry, Kaballah. I didn't know he was going to do that.

(She exits, then after a beat reenters.)

ELISE: Teach me how to do it. That raptor thing. With the stories and squawking. Teach me how to do it.

KABALLAH: You're not nice.

ELISE: I'm serious, Kaballah. I want to do that. Teach me. Please.

KABALLAH: Teach you?

ELISE: I mean — teach me to say those things you say. I've always wanted to say things like that, but I've never known how. I'm not good with words.

KABALLAH: You don't have to be good with words. It's all in the shoulders. You feel it all between your shoulder blades. You close your eyes and you have these huge leathery wings growing out of your back. You have razor sharp talons jutting out of your claws and toes. You have — you have a beak, a sharp, razor sharp beak that you rip things apart with. And you can fly. You can fly away from anything you want to, but you don't need to because you can destroy anything that you don't like. Just lean back and concentrate on your shoulder blades.

(Elise has been intently focusing on her Raptor physique. She and Kaballah breathe together, feeling their wings and talons.)

KABALLAH: What's something you don't like?

ELISE: Um . . .

KABALLAH: Don't umm! Don't open your eyes! You know. Raptors are purely instinctual. You always know exactly what to do. What don't you like? What makes you wish you could kill somebody?

ELISE: Being invisible.

KABALLAH: Being invisible. Then Raptors shall not be invisible!

ELISE: I will not be invisible! I will not be invisible!

(She and Kaballah begin to chant this until it becomes a frenzied song, with Elise beating out a complex rhythm on a nearby rock or the floor.)

ELISE: I will not be invisible/

KABALLAH: I will instead be the great Woman Raptor Beast. And watch anyone try to erase me!

ELISE: No one will erase me!

KABALLAH: They will try to erase us by making us smile.

"Oh, yeah?" we say/"Well we don't like smiling. It makes me nauseous."

ELISE: So go to hell!

KABALLAH: Go to hell!

ELISE: And don't forget/

KABALLAH: I am not devoid of fire/you touch me, I'll burn you

ELISE: But of course this dude doesn't believe me./So when he whips out a bottle of Tommy Girl from behind his greasy, acne-encrusted back/I whip out my giant Raptor claws!/Awwwk!

KABALLAH: Awwk!

ELISE: And I rake them slowly across his face/leaving him whining in a clearing in the woods/as I run/howling/into the night. Awwk!

KABALLAH: Awwk!

(Elise and Kaballah stare at each other, charged.)

Light Years
Billy Aronson

Seriocomic

Daphne and Courtney (both eighteen)

This scene takes place on the first day of freshman year at 6 P.M.

Living room of a freshman double. Door to bedroom. Door to hall. Desk
with chair. Closet. Couch. Crate. Daphne and Courtney.

DAPHNE: So if I wear these sunglasses —

COURTNEY: Philosophy.

DAPHNE: They'll see me as —

COURTNEY: Lit major, comp lit, philosophy, psych.

DAPHNE: But if I go with this pair —

COURTNEY: Engineer.

DAPHNE: Engineer.

COURTNEY: Exactly.

DAPHNE: So I have . . .

COURTNEY: The choice.

DAPHNE: Right.

COURTNEY: Deep or diligent.

    (Daphne thinks.)

COURTNEY: Or you could go to the picnic open, like me. Open to sun-
shine. Open to the breeze. Open to law school.

DAPHNE: Right.

COURTNEY: Any choice has its pluses. I'm just saying that before you get
pegged, you should decide.

DAPHNE: Right.

COURTNEY: Same goes for the photo.

DAPHNE: The photo.

COURTNEY: On your desk.

DAPHNE: Oh yeah.

COURTNEY: That photo says, to those dropping by on their way to the picnic, that you have someone, and that you're taken.

DAPHNE: Right.

COURTNEY: I have lots of someones. But I'm not taken.

DAPHNE: Right.

COURTNEY: I have friends who are taken, but want to appear untaken. That's their business.

DAPHNE: Right.

COURTNEY: I even have a friend who has no one, but wants to appear taken, for strategic purposes.

DAPHNE: Right.

COURTNEY: So anything goes. It's all up to you.

(Daphne nods.)

COURTNEY: So? Do you want to appear taken?

(Daphne thinks.)

COURTNEY: Let's work backwards. Do you have someone?

(Daphne thinks.)

COURTNEY: Have you ever had someone?

DAPHNE: This guy, we'd talk about everything, one time it was raining and there were all these sounds, the noises were us, saying and doing those things, that people say and do.

COURTNEY: So you have had someone.

DAPHNE: I can't remember.

COURTNEY: But you do want to have someone.

DAPHNE: Yes. Yes.

COURTNEY: So you'll put away the photo.

DAPHNE: Right.

COURTNEY: And the cross.

DAPHNE: The . . .

COURTNEY: Around your neck.

DAPHNE: This is a cross?

COURTNEY: It looks like a cross.

DAPHNE: Right.

COURTNEY: I'm not saying bury it, I'm just saying be aware.

DAPHNE: Aware.

COURTNEY: Of the whole question.

DAPHNE: Uh huh . . .

COURTNEY: Born again. Or the other extreme. Free spirit.

DAPHNE: Right.

COURTNEY: We're talking about your most fundamental values.

DAPHNE: My most fundamental values.

COURTNEY: Exactly.

DAPHNE: Which are . . .

COURTNEY: Pursuit of truth. Love of humanity. I don't know.

DAPHNE: Right.

COURTNEY: Before heading to the picnic you need to ask yourself: Is that
symbol rooted in the exact message you want to send out?

DAPHNE: Right.

COURTNEY: So?

DAPHNE: I'll come up with the answers as we shop for a plant.

COURTNEY: Shop for a plant? Now?

(Daphne sits frozen.)

COURTNEY: Are you telling me . . . you want to skip the freshmen picnic?

(Daphne sits frozen.)

COURTNEY: Daphne. Outside that window, in a matter of minutes, our
generation will assemble. For this chance to win a prime spot in their
ranks you've spent your last three summers serving burgers, committed your Fridays to filing periodicals, and taken out loans you'll
be repaying til you're disabled or forty or dead. So seize the moment.
Select the impression that will leap from your front and ricochet
through the crowd til you're burned in their brains as a —

DAPHNE: Philosophical lit major who's not religious and not taken.

COURTNEY: Good. So then . . .

DAPHNE: I can't put away the photo. Because I can't stand up. My legs,
something funny.

COURTNEY: Listen to me. Daphne. You'll be fine, because you're blessed
with something that will get you through no matter what the world
throws at you. You're pure.

DAPHNE: Pure what.

COURTNEY: Inside you, is a basic goodness and honesty that's special.

DAPHNE: You see this after knowing me for two hours?

COURTNEY: I saw this after knowing you for two seconds. The things I'm encouraging you to consider are icing on the cake. That's all. We just want the right icing, for so very fine a cake.

DAPHNE: *(Sitting up.)* This is all so easy for you.

COURTNEY: You think I'm the type who just, everything's easy?

DAPHNE: I didn't mean anything bad.

COURTNEY: I know you didn't. It's only that some people have tended to label me. You know. As the type. Gliding along. Not really meaning things. But the thing is, growing up, my mother couldn't be with us so I, always had to be the one smiling, but it wasn't easy always being the one smiling, people don't realize that, but I need you to know that when I say things to you I really mean those things from my heart.

DAPHNE: I know that.

COURTNEY: Anyway. Before I open the door to let in potential escorts, let's both take a second.

(They sit. A "Special Song" plays from above. Instantly, both go into a trance.)

COURTNEY: Somebody upstairs has good taste in songs.

(They listen.)

DAPHNE: Sleeping late on a snow day.

COURTNEY: Driving home from the prom.

(When the song fades, they emerge from their trances. Courtney opens the door.)

Reclaimed
Judy GeBauer

Dramatic

Vivien Fielding (late thirties); Emily Fielding, her daughter (late teens)

> Synopsis: The time is 1881. Vivien Fielding, once a captive of the
> Sioux, returned years ago to a white society unable to accept her and
> the experiences that left her face tattooed. Estranged from her straight-
> laced husband, she loses the custody of their young daughter. She
> takes to the lecture circuit, but she finds herself a kind of freak
> attraction, and she returns to the plains. This is the first time mother
> and daughter have met since her capture in the 1860s. They are in
> a rustic building once used as a trading post. Vivien is writing when
> Emily enters.

VIVIEN: If you've come about medicine, I don't have it yet. I don't know
what's happened. It's not on the train. I'll go to the fort again today.
If necessary I'll write another request. I can't give you any better —

EMILY: I'm so sorry coming in unannounced like this . . . We've never met.
(Vivien puts on spectacles.)
A rather frightening man showed me the way. I told him I wanted
to have a letter written. He said he knew someone who could write.
He said people who come here on the railroad stop here and look
at her.

VIVIEN: Is your father with you?

EMILY: I don't really need a letter written.

VIVIEN: You're here all alone?

EMILY: We're switching to the spur that connects with the Northern Pacific.

VIVIEN: Northern Pacific. Then you're traveling farther west?

EMILY: To join my husband.

VIVIEN: Husband.

EMILY: He's a partner in the Northern Pacific. A junior partner.

VIVIEN: You have a husband.

EMILY: We only have a short time while they switch us. It was wrong of me to come upon you like this . . .

VIVIEN: Oh, no, don't be embarrassed, please. I'm glad you came.

EMILY: I'm not myself.

VIVIEN: I should invite you to sit down, offer you —

EMILY: My husband's been terribly injured.

VIVIEN: I never imagined you married.

EMILY: Inspecting some coupling device. I don't know exactly.

VIVIEN: Are you faint?

EMILY: They never tell you anything.

VIVIEN: And you're traveling by yourself?

EMILY: I don't mean to trouble you with this.

VIVIEN: All this distance. All this time. How did you even know to ask for me?

EMILY: Mrs. Carrington.

VIVIEN: You've met Fanny Carrington.

EMILY: I was always going to write to you. I was always starting to write. But I never knew what to say. This is how your voice sounds.

VIVIEN: This little place used to be a trading post.

EMILY: Do you remember the oil portrait of you in our house?

VIVIEN: Imagine a single building on the plains, long before —

EMILY: Papa ordered that painting taken down.

VIVIEN: I speak English and Lakotah. The People needed so many things when I came, the Army didn't have supplies enough. The People didn't know how to ask for anything. Now and then I write letters . . . some of the soldiers can't . . . spell . . .

EMILY: I asked Papa why. He said, "This is not your mother's face."

VIVIEN: He was wrong. That was your mother's face.

EMILY: He forgets sometimes. He calls me Vivien. Am I what you imagined?

(Emily picks up and handles a carved wooden toy wolf.)

VIVIEN: That belonged to your sister.

EMILY: Oh. My sister. Yes.

VIVIEN: It was made for her by her father.

EMILY: Is your Indian family here with you?

VIVIEN: The People were moved to Pine Ridge some time ago.

EMILY: Why didn't you move with them?

VIVIEN: I don't belong with them.

EMILY: Did you carry her on your back?

VIVIEN: Yes.

EMILY: And nurse her in the Indian way?

VIVIEN: In the usual way.

EMILY: Adam doesn't want to have children right away.

VIVIEN: Your sister was a baby when I left her. I would never see her again, so I thought. I believed I was going to spend the rest of my life with you. I don't need a keepsake of you.

EMILY: Adam thinks when people have children too soon they surrender their own youth.

VIVIEN: Do you want someone to go with you?

EMILY: I don't even know where I'm going. The Columbia River, wherever that is.

VIVIEN: Emily, shall I go with you?

EMILY: We weren't meant to be a family like other families.

VIVIEN: I'm so glad you came. So glad.

(Vivien takes Emily's hand and examines the wedding ring. Emily touches the scars on Vivien's cheeks.)

EMILY: That must have been awful.

(Emily starts to leave.)

Don't the Sioux have some notion about choosing special friends and people like that?

VIVIEN: How did you know about that?

EMILY: I read about Indian customs somewhere. "Farewell to My Daughters," I think it was called.

VIVIEN: It's a custom they call hunka (hoong KAH).

EMILY: That was the word. I didn't know how to pronounce it.

VIVIEN: It means to choose a special relative.

EMILY: I suppose there's a ceremony.

VIVIEN: A long one.

EMILY: Well, I'm the impatient sort. I can't stand ceremonies and rituals and things. Getting married was the worst ordeal, but Papa would have every detail. So let me just say, I choose you. You are the mother I choose. And if I never see you again, I choose you.

(Silence.)

Adam says this railroad is a beginning. He says men will ride up in the air one day. See the Earth from the sky. Not just balloons. Real air machines. Won't that be an extraordinary thing? I say women will ride in the sky, too. Adam says no. Do you realize in just nineteen more years there will come a whole new century? I'm going to live in it. Won't I have a lot to tell.

(Silence.)

You called me Emily.

Relative Strangers
Sheri Wilner

Dramatic

Marie Barrett (midtwenties); Marie Harvey (midfifties)

> A young airline passenger, Marie Barrett, decides that the woman
> seated next to her, Marie Harvey, might be the mother she never had.

MARIE HARVEY: They really pile us on top of each other . . . *(Indicates seat
belt.)* and strap us down. If they truly want to "ensure our comfort,"
they wouldn't strap us down.

MARIE BARRETT: Don't they have to? For safety's sake?

MARIE HARVEY: Do you feel safe bound up like a prisoner? I sure as hell
don't.

MARIE BARRETT: Planes scare me no matter what.

(Marie Harvey returns to her magazine.)

MARIE HARVEY: Don't worry. You're safer up here than you are down there.

MARIE BARRETT: Do you live in New York?

MARIE HARVEY: I live about an hour's drive from Manhattan. Twenty minutes if you walk.

MARIE BARRETT: I've only lived there for three years. I'm originally from
Rhode Island.

MARIE HARVEY: Quite a change.

MARIE BARRETT: Yeah, it was. The biggest I've made.

MARIE HARVEY: There'll be bigger.

MARIE BARRETT: What's the biggest change you've made?

MARIE HARVEY: I used to be your age. Now I'm mine.

MARIE BARRETT: Are you going to Charleston for anything special?

MARIE HARVEY: Not special. No.

MARIE BARRETT: Just visiting?

MARIE HARVEY: Just divorcing. My divorce hearing is tomorrow.

MARIE BARRETT: Your family lives in Charleston?

MARIE HARVEY: Just my husband. Divorcing me isn't enough. He also needed to move to a different climactic region.

MARIE BARRETT: I'm sorry.

MARIE HARVEY: Don't be. We had ten happy years of marriage . . . which isn't bad out of twenty-five.

MARIE BARRETT: You were married that long?

MARIE HARVEY: Yeah, well, what's twenty-five years?

MARIE BARRETT: Me. My birthday was last month.

MARIE HARVEY: Well I hope the past twenty-five years have brought you more happiness than they've brought me.

MARIE BARRETT: I don't know that they have.

MARIE HARVEY: Unless the only things you have to show for them are bills from your lawyer and a tan line on your ring finger, I'd say they have.

MARIE BARRETT: Are those really the only things you have? Bills and — ?

MARIE HARVEY: And in a couple of weeks I won't even have a tan line.

MARIE BARRETT: You don't have any children?

MARIE HARVEY: I didn't say that.

MARIE BARRETT: Oh. So you do have something.

MARIE HARVEY: Divorces don't allow for much neutrality. At least not in my family. Good news is, if you know anyone at Hallmark, you can tell 'em to make one less Mother's Day card this year.

(Marie Barrett stares sympathetically at Marie Harvey. Marie Harvey tries to ignore her for as long as she can and then:)

MARIE HARVEY: Yes?

MARIE BARRETT: If you want to talk about anything, I'm a great listener. I wouldn't mind at all. Really. I don't know much about divorce, but I know a lot about being alone. Would you like to talk about being alone?

MARIE HARVEY: Not at the moment. Maybe when we reach cruising altitude.

MARIE BARRETT: Well you know where to find me.

(Marie Barrett returns to her book. Marie Harvey tries to read her magazine, but she keeps looking at Marie Barrett as if she wants to say something.)

MARIE HARVEY: Um . . . excuse me — .

MARIE BARRETT: Yes?

MARIE HARVEY: Nothing, I'm sorry.

MARIE BARRETT: No, no. Did you want to talk about something?

MARIE HARVEY: No. I — .

MARIE BARRETT: Go ahead. I'm listening.

MARIE HARVEY: It's just, well, I can't help it, the mother in me wants to tell you to turn the light on while you're reading.

(A call button "bing" is heard, indicating a "passenger" requesting service.)

MARIE BARRETT: What did you say?

MARIE HARVEY: You should turn the light on. You're destroying your eyes —.

MARIE BARRETT: No, no before that. What did you say before that?

MARIE HARVEY: Nothing.

MARIE BARRETT: No. Something. "The mother in me." Right?

MARIE HARVEY: Yeah . . .

MARIE BARRETT: That's what I thought. Wow.

MARIE HARVEY: What?

MARIE BARRETT: Wow.

MARIE HARVEY: What?!

MARIE BARRETT: I'm just going to seize the opportunity, OK? Because who knows when it will ever come my way again.

MARIE HARVEY: I don't know what you're talking about.

MARIE BARRETT: I'll throw out a bunch of questions and you can answer them one at a time . . . or pick and choose the ones you want — whatever feels right — Just go wherever "the mother" in you takes you, OK? All right, this is it.

(Taking a deep breath.)

Would you definitely say it's better to breast-feed a baby? Does the fork go on the left or the right? Um . . . oh yea — is it true you can't wear white until after Memorial Day? and should you really wait an hour after eating to swim? Um . . . damn, why haven't I been writing these down? I literally have hundreds — *thousands* of — . Oh, I know, if an invitation says "and guest" —

MARIE HARVEY: I just thought you should turn your light on. *(She reaches over Marie Barrett's head and turns on her light.)* That's all.

MARIE BARRETT: I know you must think I'm a weirdo, but I'm not. I don't have a mother, you see. It's something I'm aware of every second of the day. Like if I didn't have any arms or legs . . . or skin. She died during childbirth. They say as soon as I emerged — as soon as I took my first breath, she took her last. She really was only a vessel for me if you think about it — just like this plane. She received me, took me to a destination, and then I emerged, disembarked and she was gone. Lame metaphor I know, but the mind — my mind — needs ways to understand, to make sense. I'm always feeling so . . . lost — like everyone in the world has a map that I don't have. Sometimes I find I just don't know how to get around. Like there's vital information I don't have access to. Letters missing from my alphabet, you know?

But now, all of a sudden . . . here you are. I know this is lousy timing given your situation, but there's too much I need to know. So I'm just gonna grab a hold of this before it floats away. OK?

MARIE HARVEY: I don't think so.

MARIE BARRETT: But you offered — .

MARIE HARVEY: I didn't offer anything.

MARIE BARRETT: Yes you did.

MARIE HARVEY: No I didn't.

(Beat.)

MARIE BARRETT: How many children did you say you have?

MARIE HARVEY: I didn't.

MARIE BARRETT: Sons?

(Marie Harvey shakes her head no.

Daughters. How many?

MARIE HARVEY: Enough.

(Marie Harvey flips through her magazine. Pause.)

MARIE BARRETT: My name's Marie. What's yours?

(No response.)

OK — I'll guess.

MARIE HARVEY: *(Before she can guess.)* Marie.

MARIE BARRETT: Yes?

MARIE HARVEY: No. That's my name too. Marie.

MARIE BARRETT: Is that the truth? Is it?

MARIE HARVEY: Yes.

MARIE BARRETT: That's . . . phenomenal. My God! Can you believe it? Maybe that's how they seat us.

(Marie Harvey looks at her magazine.)

Marie, there's something I really need to ask you — .

MARIE HARVEY: Look, I don't know you — .

MARIE BARRETT: My name is Marie Barrett. I live in Brooklyn, I'm twenty-five years old, I'm Episcopalian. I work for a small but reputable publishing company and . . . um . . . I'm allergic to birch trees. What else do you want to know?

MARIE HARVEY: I shouldn't have said anything about the light.

MARIE BARRETT: The mother in you couldn't help it.

MARIE HARVEY: Marie, in twenty-four hours I have to stand in front of a judge and a bunch of other strangers and bicker with my husband about how much of an allowance he'll give me per month so at forty-nine years old, and having acquired no marketable skills, I won't have to beg anyone to give me my first job — .

MARIE BARRETT: You've never had a job?

MARIE HARVEY: I paint.

Relative Strangers
Sheri Wilner

Dramatic

Marie Barrett (midtwenties); Marie Harvey (midfifties)

> A young airline passenger, Marie Barrett, decides that the woman seated next to her, Marie Harvey, might be the mother she never had.

MARIE BARRETT: I wouldn't bother you like this if I hadn't been waiting what feels like my whole entire life to ask someone this quest — .

MARIE HARVEY: In approximately five minutes, this Bloody Mary will kick in, allowing me to pretend I don't have to do tomorrow what I have to do tomorrow. So if I enlighten you with some motherly advice now, you'll leave me alone for the rest of the flight, agreed? Minimal interaction only, right? Right?

MARIE BARRETT: Well, I might — .

MARIE HARVEY: I'll sweeten the deal. Stop asking questions and the entire armrest is yours. OK? Maternal advice. Here goes — *(Taking a drink.)* If you *have* to get married, marry a lawyer . . . surround yourself with people you can tolerate but don't particularly like and most importantly — never, *never* have any children. Lovely meeting you — have a good trip. *(She turns away.)*

MARIE BARRETT: Why shouldn't I have kids? Because I didn't have a mother of my own? Am I missing something essential that all other women have? Like some internal instruction book?

MARIE HARVEY: Just do what I did — read Dr. Spock and then hire a nanny. *(She takes another gulp of her drink.)*

MARIE BARRETT: *(Laughs.)* Did your daughter inherit your sense of humor?

MARIE HARVEY: No, just my nervous condition.

MARIE BARRETT: I see.

MARIE HARVEY: You see? Really? What do you see? Do I have an I've-driven-my-child-to-seek-extensive-psychotherapy look to me? I've also driven her to an aromatherapist, a scalp masseuse, an herbalist, a dog psychologist . . . an astrologist . . . and a marriage counselor. And every Goddamn one of them tells her it's all my fault.

MARIE BARRETT: Even the dog psychologist?

MARIE HARVEY: Apparently even little Snowflake isn't immune to the tension my visits create.

MARIE BARRETT: *(Laughs.)* You're really very funny.

MARIE HARVEY: Well, I'm glad you've enjoyed our little time together. *(Lifting her class in a toast.)* Good-bye.

MARIE BARRETT: I have enjoyed it. That's actually what I wanted to ask you about. You see, I always hoped I could find someone . . . like you . . . who I could talk to from time to time. You know, like if I have any questions, maybe I could call you — .

MARIE HARVEY: What?

MARIE BARRETT: I'm just so tired of never knowing where to find answers. I need someone . . . a woman . . . an older woman, who I can get to when I need help — .

MARIE HARVEY: Are you asking me to be your mother?

MARIE BARRETT: No. *(Beat.)* It would be more like freelancing.

MARIE HARVEY: Good God — don't give yourself away to a stranger.

MARIE BARRETT: See — you're giving me advice already — you're a natural.

MARIE HARVEY: *(Uneasily.)* You're going too far. Now leave me alone.

MARIE BARRETT: I don't mean to imply that I'd call you constantly, just on occasion — .

MARIE HARVEY: *(Overlapping.)* I'm not listening to this.

MARIE BARRETT: We both live in New York. We could meet for coffee from time to time.

MARIE HARVEY: Stop it.

MARIE BARRETT: Your own daughter would have first dibs of course, but we could all work out a schedule I'm sure —

MARIE HARVEY: Not another word.

MARIE BARRETT: Only when it's — .

MARIE HARVEY: *I mean it!*

MARIE BARRETT: I'm sorry. This isn't a good time for you.

(Marie Harvey finishes her drink, shakes the ice around her glass, then looks up and down the aisle.)

I spend so much time trying to acquire family I can't imagine having to give any up. I'm sorry.

MARIE HARVEY: Don't be. My husband and I were happy for twenty years. And then we met.

(Marie Barrett does not laugh.)

MARIE HARVEY: *(Imitating a rim-shot.)* Ba-dump-ump.

MARIE BARRETT: Would you like to talk about how you're feeling?

MARIE HARVEY: I'm feeling annoyed.

MARIE BARRETT: I mean about your divorce. Would you like to talk about that?

MARIE HARVEY: Yes. But to someone I've known for longer than five minutes.

MARIE BARRETT: Well that's unfair.

MARIE HARVEY: What is unfair?

MARIE BARRETT: Shutting me out like that. It's not my fault we've only known each other for five minutes.

MARIE HARVEY: You shouldn't take it personally. I don't like talking to strangers.

MARIE BARRETT: Why?

MARIE HARVEY: Because they end up asking you to be their mother.

MARIE BARRETT: This has happened to you before? Has it?

MARIE HARVEY: I was speaking figuratively.

MARIE BARRETT: That's a relief. You're the first person I've asked. It would be just my luck if you had like a waiting list or something.

MARIE HARVEY: *I'm* the first person?

MARIE BARRETT: Yes.

MARIE HARVEY: Why on earth would *I* be the first person you've asked?

MARIE BARRETT: Because of what you said — "the mother in me." You saw me reading in the dark and the nurturer in you was so strong you couldn't resist reaching out to me. I'm a perfect stranger but you wanted to take care of me, to protect me. You're who I've been searching for. You've got the right stuff.

MARIE HARVEY: I don't have any stuff.

MARIE BARRETT: Exactly. You're alone like me. I mean, you're going to get divorced tomorrow, and no one's coming with you. It seems like . . .

maybe . . . you have no one to ask. *(Beat.)* Hey — would you like me to go with you?

MARIE HARVEY: What?!

MARIE BARRETT: You don't want to be there alone, do you?

MARIE HARVEY: Thanks, but no thanks. Maybe next time.

MARIE BARRETT: I think you're looking for someone as much as I am.

MARIE HARVEY: Oh God, I'm in hell, I'm in sheer hell.

MARIE BARRETT: Truthfully, I don't believe for a second that you want me to stop talking to you.

MARIE HARVEY: Then make believe. Please.

Shoot
David Cirone

Seriocomic

Nikki (seventeen); Sondra (seventeen)

> Sondra and Nikki — high school seniors and best friends — are out-
> casts at their school, where the "Preps" ridicule and provoke them
> because of their punk hairstyles, clothes, and piercings. Sondra's been
> a shoo-in for valedictorian, until a bad grade from Mr. Malcolm
> brings her down to number four. They're sitting on the back porch
> of Nikki's home in North Carolina, watching TV, smoking pot, and
> throwing "hate rocks" at the clothesline.

NIKKI: You know what I hate?
SONDRA: *(In a bad mood.)* Me, too!
NIKKI: What?
SONDRA: What?
NIKKI: You don't even know what I'm gonna say.
SONDRA: Say it, I bet I hate it!
NIKKI: I was gonna say I hate homeroom.
SONDRA: Oh yeah, I definitely hate homeroom!
NIKKI: Yeah, it fucking sucks!
　　(She throws a rock. It hits a towel hanging on the line.)
SONDRA: You know what I hate?
NIKKI: What? No wait. "Me, too!"
SONDRA: What?
NIKKI: Just like you. I know I'm gonna hate it.
SONDRA: *(Looks back at TV.)* I hate this talk show!
　　(Sondra throws a rock.)
NIKKI: *(Turning around.)* Jenny Jones? No way! I love Jenny Jones!
SONDRA: See? *(Loud, superior.)* Ha-ha!
NIKKI: Ha-ha what?
SONDRA: You blew it! Too fast.

NIKKI: I did not!

SONDRA: I hate Jenny Jones and you don't, but you started to say you did.

NIKKI: So?

SONDRA: So you jumped the gun! It's called being "impetuous."

NIKKI: Whatever . . .

SONDRA: "Incogitant."

NIKKI: What-ever! *(Looks at TV.)* Ooh! Look! Did you see that?

SONDRA: What?

NIKKI: That woman just slapped that guy right in the face!

SONDRA: *(Sarcastic.)* No. Missed it. Sure it was thrilling.

NIKKI: *(Turning on her, irritated.)* Well, you know what I hate? People who say things like that, like "jump the gun." What does that even mean? Like my mom saying "shoot" all the time, trying to be nice — if you wanna say "shit," say "shit"! Shit shit shit! I hate that!

SONDRA: Me too! *(They both throw rocks.)* Why is your brother watching that?

NIKKI: Let him watch it. Least he ain't out here bugging us.

SONDRA: When are they coming back?

NIKKI: I don't know.

SONDRA: This is like, late for them, isn't it?

NIKKI: No. Not really. They're out late a lot lately. A lot.

SONDRA: That's fucked up, sticking you with your brother.

NIKKI: Fucked up is right!

SONDRA: Doesn't he go out?

NIKKI: "Not allowed."

SONDRA: He can't leave the house?

NIKKI: We can't leave the house.

SONDRA: We?

NIKKI: Ain't that some shit?

SONDRA: That doesn't make any sense. Where're you gonna go? Out in the woods?

NIKKI: Nowhere! There's nowhere to go! It's just their fucking game while they screw around on each other. They keep telling us about their "special close friends," but it's like — come on! I know what's going on, it's not like . . .

SONDRA: Oh, they've got "friends"?

NIKKI: Yeah, "friends"! See — that's what I'm talking about! I'm seven-teen — they think I don't know what "friends" means? I hate that! *(She throws a rock.)* Man!

SONDRA: That's stupid.

NIKKI: *(Quick.)* Hey! Don't call me stupid! Miss GPA!

SONDRA: No, I mean — it's stupid to make you stay in the house! There's nowhere for you to go. Nowhere bad.

NIKKI: Look, I don't give a shit. They leave, fine. They leave me alone, they leave me money, I smoke out here whenever I want. I just look . . . at the fucking . . . woods . . .

SONDRA: Yeah . . . *(They share the joint.)* I don't think I hate the woods.

NIKKI: Me either.

SONDRA: But I hate . . . the number four.

NIKKI: *(Laughs a little.)* Yeah! I bet you do! *(Pause.)* Hey. Throw.

SONDRA: Oh, yeah. *(Sondra throws another rock.)* Where's Rach?

NIKKI: I don't know. Coming. She said she was, when we left work.

SONDRA: That was a while ago.

NIKKI: She'll be here. She called.

SONDRA: That why you're listening to this shit again? For Rach?

NIKKI: I've had this CD forever!

SONDRA: You were so over them like last year . . .

NIKKI: So what?

SONDRA: *(Teasing.)* So — You know . . .

NIKKI: No, I don't know.

SONDRA: Yeah you do.

NIKKI: What are you talking about? *(Turns and bangs on the window.)* J.T.! Go to bed! It's eleven o'clock! *(She watches for a second, then sits back down.)* Is it eleven yet?

SONDRA: Yeah. Almost. Something like that.

NIKKI: *(Glances over shoulder.)* Aw, man! Little fucker left the TV on! *(Shouts.)* Dammit, J.T.! *(Sits.)* Whatever. I ain't paying the bills.

SONDRA: Hey.

NIKKI: What?

SONDRA: I'm right about Rach. Just admit it.

NIKKI: *(Irritated.)* Just shut up about that, OK?

SONDRA: Does she know?

NIKKI: What?

SONDRA: That you like her!

NIKKI: Sondra . . . ? What?

SONDRA: You like her.

NIKKI: Get the fuck outta here!

SONDRA: *(On a roll.)* I mean it's fucked up that you can't tell her. Senior year and all . . . *(No response.)* Madonna's a lesbian . . .

NIKKI: Madonna's bi.

SONDRA: So, she's still a lesbian.

NIKKI: I'm not Madonna!

SONDRA: You should tell her!

NIKKI: Just — Sondra, I mean — just shut up, OK? Don't say anything.

SONDRA: OK.

NIKKI: I mean it. Number four!

SONDRA: Hey!

NIKKI: Well, then shut up about Rach!

SONDRA: OK! Bitch!

NIKKI: Slut!

SONDRA: Whore!

NIKKI: Cunt!

SONDRA: Skank!

NIKKI: Fish! *(Suddenly excited.)* Aw, man! You know who smelled like fish the other day? Maylene! In P.E.! I thought I was gonna just fall out!

SONDRA: *(Laughs.)* I hate her! Really! She always smells like fish!

NIKKI: What is she, number one now?

SONDRA: Hey! I said shut up about that!

NIKKI: Sorry, sorry. *(Pause.)* But, really — I'm sorry about that. You got robbed.

SONDRA: Whatever.

NIKKI: You did! I mean, what's up with Mr. Malcolm?

SONDRA: I don't know.

NIKKI: I can't believe he'd turn on you like that. I thought he was so cool!

SONDRA: Thought. Coulda. Shoulda. Woulda. Whatever!

NIKKI: You and Rach hang out with him all the time!

SONDRA: Well, he's full of shit.

NIKKI: Right? Just like my fucking parents. You shouldn't ever speak to
   him again.

SONDRA: Not planning on it.

NIKKI: Next time he says, "Hey, you wanna smoke?" I'm gonna be like,
   "No way! You suck!"

SONDRA: Yeah.

NIKKI: He totally sucks. I'd waste his ass!

SONDRA: *(Laughs.)* Yeah! Thought about it.

NIKKI: Yeah?

SONDRA: Crossed my mind once or twice today.

NIKKI: Fuckin' A! Mr. Malcolm gets a rock.

Speaking in Tongues
Andrew Bovell

Dramatic

Sonja (thirties to forties); Jane (thirties to forties)

> Sonja has come to this bar by herself. There, she strikes up a con-
> versation with a woman named Jane who, it turns out, is having an
> affair with Sonja's husband.

> *A bar. The lights are low. Sonja is on the dance floor moving to the music
> in a slow, sensuous sway. Jane is sitting at a table sipping a drink. She's
> watching Sonja dance. She feels embarrassed by the sight of a woman
> dancing alone but at the same time she admires her audacity. The music
> fades. Sonja stands in stillness for a moment, then looks over to Jane.
> Jane looks away.*

SONJA: Are you curious or just rude?

JANE: I'm sorry.

SONJA: Was I making a fool of myself?

JANE: What?

SONJA: Dancing by myself.

JANE: No.

SONJA: Good.

JANE: On the contrary, I'm envious. I love to dance. I just don't have
the . . . courage to get up by myself.

SONJA: That probably means you just haven't had enough to drink.

JANE: Maybe.

SONJA: I just stopped in for the one but it tasted so good that two seemed
like a good idea and three is so close to two that you hardly notice
the difference and four, well it comes after three.

JANE: Four and I'd be flat on my back.

SONJA: You wish. *(Beat.)* I'm sorry. My tongue slipped beyond my control on margarita number three.

JANE: Then maybe you should have stopped on number two.

SONJA: That suits you.

JANE: What?

SONJA: Disapproval. You do it well.

JANE: I'm sorry.

SONJA: You must be somebody's mother.

JANE: No. I'm not.

SONJA: Oh. I'm sorry.

JANE: Why are you apologizing?

SONJA: Because you are.

JANE: Am I? Sorry. I think it's something women do.

SONJA: Yes. When they have low self-esteem. It's an affliction. *(Beat . . . tension.)* Look, I don't know what you're doing here, in a place like this, but I'm here because my life is falling apart in ways I never thought were possible. So I've come here, against all my better judgment, my stupid idiotic better judgment, to forget.

JANE: And have you forgotten?

SONJA: No. The bastard is still on my mind.

JANE: Ah . . . we have that in common. My name's Jane. *(Beat.)*

SONJA: Jane . . . That's a nice name Jane.

JANE: It's a common name. It's an unextraordinary name. It suits me well.

SONJA: Do you mean that?

JANE: Plain Jane.

SONJA: You're not plain.

JANE: Thanks.

SONJA: So . . . your bastard, he's your husband?

JANE: That's the one.

SONJA: You've left him?

JANE: Does it show?

SONJA: You have a certain look.

JANE: What, bitter?

SONJA: No. Excited. Full of anticipation. Full of hope. Full of potential.

JANE: Wasted potential.

SONJA: How?

JANE: I had plans. As a younger woman I had great plans.

SONJA: What, life's over? You've just left your husband . . .

JANE: Actually —

SONJA: Life's just about to begin.

JANE: He left me.

SONJA: Ah . . . it's better to be the one who leaves. Your family and friends start to hate you and that's strangely liberating.

JANE: I would have left, but my husband's a gentleman. He's always doing the right thing, I never get the chance.

SONJA: My husband never does the right thing. But he's a bit slow off the mark. I tend to move quicker than him.

JANE: Have you left him?

SONJA: Yes.

JANE: For good?

SONJA: For now. *(Beat.)* Look at me. *(Jane does.)* What do you see?

JANE: A woman?

SONJA: A woman of middle age.

JANE: Yes.

SONJA: A woman of some accomplishment. A woman at the height of her powers. Not her beauty. She was once more beautiful. I've begun to age. But I feel all right about that. I like the lines around my eyes. I like the shape of my stomach. I'm not sure if he does though. I have two degrees. I have a wonderful job. I have my own money. I have two children.

JANE: You have everything.

SONJA: I don't have a husband who wants me.

JANE: Does that cancel out all the rest?

SONJA: No, I want it all.

JANE: You have children.

SONJA: I have children.

JANE: You left them? *(Beat.)*

SONJA: No, I left my husband.

JANE: But who's looking after them?

SONJA: He's looking after them. And they're looking after themselves. They're not babies.

JANE: I couldn't do that.

SONJA: Do you have children?

JANE: No.

SONJA: Then how do you know?

JANE: I'm sorry. It's not my business.

SONJA: But you don't approve.

JANE: It's not my place to approve or disapprove.

SONJA: But you just can't help yourself.

JANE: I guess I would have asked him to leave. If that was the case, I would have stayed.

SONJA: But I needed the time, not him. I needed the distance from him. And from my children.

JANE: I can't understand that.

SONJA: That's because you don't have children. For you they're still something unknown, desired, precious.

JANE: They're not precious to you?

SONJA: *(Hesitating.)* I love them, but precious? I have two teenage boys. Young men really. They eat. They sleep. They create a lot of washing. It's good for them that I'm not there. And it's good for me that I'm not there. And it's good for my husband. He might not think so, but it is. What are you doing here, Jane?

JANE: I don't know what I'm doing here.

SONJA: Are you here looking for company? I mean a man.

JANE: I suppose I am but I don't like to admit it.

SONJA: Then maybe I should leave.

JANE: Don't . . . I mean I don't like sitting by myself. Do you mind? *(Sonja stays.)* I met a guy here a couple of nights ago. We spent the night together and I guess I was hoping . . .

SONJA: You might run into him again.

JANE: Yeah.

SONJA: Did you get his number?

JANE: No. Is that what you do?

SONJA: Well, I'm no expert, but if you liked him.

JANE: We had agreed that it was just a once off thing. He's married as well.

SONJA: Did you get his name?

JANE: Leon. *(Sonja is silent. She masks the pain and the irony.)*

SONJA: Did you like him?

JANE: Yes.

SONJA: You want to see him again?

JANE: Yes.

SONJA: Was he good in bed?

JANE: You're very direct.

SONJA: Not always. Go on, you can tell me. It's just us here. Was he good?

JANE: Well, he made love to me like my husband used to. Once.

SONJA: My husband used to make love to me like that too. Once.

JANE: It was . . .

SONJA: Passionate.

JANE: Yes. It was . . .

SONJA: What?

JANE: Complete. *(Beat.)*

SONJA: How nice for you. And did this Leon talk about his wife?

JANE: Yes he did.

SONJA: And he's not happy?

JANE: I don't really know . . . He's still in love with her. That's why it was only going to be a one-night thing.

SONJA: But you came back, just for a second go.

JANE: I don't know why I came back. He said he couldn't imagine living without her. Which is funny because I spend most of my life imagining what it would be like to live without my husband.

SONJA: Is he that bad?

JANE: No. He's fine. It's me. I'm the miserable one. You see I'm middle-aged too. But I don't have children. I don't have a good job. I don't have money of my own. And I don't like the lines around my eyes or the shape of my stomach. And I'm scared.

SONJA: What of.

JANE: Change. *(Pause.)*

SONJA: I'm sorry. *(Pause.)*

JANE: What's wrong?

SONJA: Nothing.

JANE: You're crying.

SONJA: It's the cigarette smoke.

JANE: You're crying.

SONJA: Yeah, I'm crying.

JANE: Why?

SONJA: Because I'm Sonja . . . Leon's wife.

JANE: I know. *(Sonja looks at her. Hold. Jane starts to go.)*

SONJA: Jane.

JANE: Don't say anything. It's best. Don't you think? *(Jane leaves. Music. Sonja starts to dance.)*

Tristan
Don Nigro

Dramatic

Alison (nineteen); Sarah (seventeen)

> In the autumn of 1887, Alison has appeared mysteriously in a thunderstorm at the rather Gothic and now somewhat decaying Pendragon house in east Ohio. She's been brought in out of the rain by Rhys (seventeen), son of Gavin Rose, the owner of the house, and is now staying with the family. She can't seem to remember who she is or where she's come from, but it's clear to Sarah (seventeen), the family cook and housekeeper, that Rhys is already hopelessly in love with Alison. Sarah and Rhys have grown up together and played doctor in the bath, and Sarah has always been in love with Rhys. She is always threatening to leave the Roses, and the huge house that's much too big for her to take care of, but she loves them, and can't bring herself to go. The appearance of the beautiful Alison has dashed Sarah's hopes of ending up with Rhys, and Sarah resents her very much, and she suspects her motives. What the family doesn't know yet is that Alison is the daughter of a former servant in the house by Rhys' grandfather John Pendragon, and she has been carefully schooled by her mother to return and claim her inheritance by whatever means necessary. Alison is torn between her desire to get back the house and her growing affection for the people who live there.

Sarah is making bread in the kitchen, slamming things around, irritated.

SARAH: Struts around this house like the Queen of England. Thinks she can order me about. Doesn't do a lick of work. Just who does she think she his? Ought to throw her back out in the rain and lock the door, if you ask me. But nobody asks me. Nobody ever asks me.

ALISON: *(Coming into the kitchen.)* Can I help you with that, Sarah?

SARAH: No.

ALISON: I know how to make bread.

SARAH: Then you can see I don't need any help.

ALISON: Why do you always avoid me?

SARAH: I don't avoid you. I haven't got time to avoid you. I've got work to do. Unlike some people around here.

ALISON: I offer to help, but you won't let me.

SARAH: If you want to help, stop bothering me.

ALISON: Sarah, why don't you like me?

SARAH: It's not my job to like you.

ALISON: Is it your job to hate me?

SARAH: There's got to be a better way for you to waste your precious time than worrying about what I think of you.

ALISON: It's not a very Christian thing to hate somebody you hardly know.

SARAH: Hate is a very Christian thing. Read your Bible.

ALISON: I've read my Bible, and it doesn't say anything about hate being Christian. It says the opposite.

SARAH: Clearly you've only been reading selected parts.

ALISON: What does that mean?

SARAH: It means it's dangerous to listen to what people say unless you're also watching what they do while they're saying it.

ALISON: You're a rather clever person, aren't you?

SARAH: What business have I got being clever? I'm just a poor servant girl.

ALISON: How long have you been here?

SARAH: All my life. My mother was housekeeper here before me. I don't know how she stood it. Sometimes I get so furious at them. But she took it all in stride — Mr. Rose and his brooding, Mrs. Rose and her bouts of lunacy, and cranky old Aunt Margaret — you're lucky that one did you the favor of expiring before you arrived. She was a handful. And Rhys and I were a handful as well, I suppose, when we were children. My mother died two years ago — we wore her out, is what happened. And I took over.

ALISON: But you couldn't have been more than fifteen then.

SARAH: I don't see what that signifies. Somebody had to do it. Anyway, I won't be here much longer. I should have left when Mother died. I don't know why I didn't.

ALISON: Maybe you felt sorry for them.

SARAH: They don't need me to feel sorry for them. They can do that for themselves. Besides, they've got a big house and some money left in the bank, and they still own half the town. I'll be out of here just as soon as they can find somebody else stupid enough to come and live in this godforsaken place.

ALISON: I don't see why that should be a problem. It's lovely out here.

SARAH: In town, they think the house is haunted, and the mistress is crazy, and they tell darker stories than that.

ALISON: What kind of stories?

SARAH: Why are you bothering me with all these foolish questions? Why don't you go bother Rhys? I'm sure he'll be happy to tell you any sort of rubbish you want to hear. The two of you get along so famously together.

ALISON: Sarah, I hope you're not jealous.

SARAH: Jealous of what?

ALISON: Of Rhys and me.

SARAH: What have I got to be jealous about?

ALISON: Well, you two are good friends, aren't you? You grew up together.

SARAH: You forget, I'm just the servant girl.

ALISON: I think you're a great deal more than that.

SARAH: You don't know anything about it.

ALISON: I was hoping you and I could be friends.

SARAH: Why would you want to be friends with me? I'm just —

ALISON: Just a poor little servant girl, yes, I know, we've heard that sad lament quite enough, thank you, but it doesn't get my sympathy.

SARAH: Who asked for your damned sympathy? And what the hell would you know about being a servant?

ALISON: My mother was a servant once.

SARAH: Well, what do you want? An award?

ALISON: You really do hate me.

SARAH: I don't think anything about you, except that you mean extra clothes to wash, food to cook, dishes to rinse, you drive me berserk in the kitchen, and when Rhys is around you he acts like he's feebleminded.

ALISON: You're in love with Rhys.

SARAH: Now that has got to be the single most idiotic thing I've heard in my life. And that's saying quite a lot, living, as I do, with Mrs. Rose.

You needn't worry about me, honey. I'm no competition for you in that area.

ALISON: What did you do? Play doctor together?

SARAH: What we played is none of your business.

ALISON: I didn't come here to be your enemy, Sarah.

SARAH: Why exactly DID you come here?

ALISON: I'll tell you what I'm going to do. I'm going to help you around the house from now on, whether you like it or not.

SARAH: I don't want your help. You'll just get in the way.

ALISON: Here. I'll break the beans.

SARAH: You just keep your hands off my beans.

(Alison sits down and begins breaking beans.)

ALISON: You and I are going to be great friends in the end, Sarah. Really great friends, I think.

SARAH: Don't hold your breath.

Scenes for
Two Men

Actor!
Frederick Stroppel

Comic

Actor (twenties to thirties); Publicist (any age)

> This play is a mordantly funny satire of the absurd world of the actor.
> It follows an actor's life, from birth till The End. Here, Our Hero is
> hustled by a fast-talking publicist.

Actor takes a seat on an airplane.

ACTOR: Flying back to L.A., I'm filled with misgivings. I know that getting involved with Pinky would touch off a scandal that would do
wonders for my career. But is this what it's all about? Publicity at all
costs? I keep thinking back to Taylor. You know, maybe she was right.
What happened to my talent? What happened to all that bright
promise? I mean, look at all the people I've slept with, and I'm still
doing TV movies. There has to be a better way.

(A Publicist sits down beside the actor.)

PUBLICIST: Talking to yourself, chief? *(Offers his hand.)* Marty Herring.
I'm a publicist for FailSafe Films. Caught you on *Cabot and Pinky*
this morning. You're got something I like. I don't know what it is,
but you've got it.

ACTOR: Thank you.

PUBLICIST: Got a proposition for you, and think hard before you say yes.
It concerns — well, let me beat around the bush a little first. We
have a big star in our stable, you've probably heard of her — Cassidy Velour.

ACTOR: Cassidy Velour, of course. Everyone's heard of . . .

PUBLICIST: Let me finish, please. We have a very good relationship with
Cassidy. Three films in the can, a first-look deal with her produc-
tion company, this summer she's opening in a major romantic comedy opposite Mr. Tom Hanks — terrific movie; they fall in love, she
goes into a coma, there's a dog . . .

ACTOR: I can't wait to see it.

PUBLICIST: Me, too. Should be a humongous runaway hit. Unless . . .

ACTOR: Unless what?

PUBLICIST: Well, we've got a little problem. You know how it is with romantic movies — lots of kissing, lots of implied sex, a little obvious sex; Cassidy actually flashes a little tit in this movie, and it's quite sumptuous. But all of this kissy-sexy stuff requires a certain agreement with the audience, an understanding of who's who, and what's what, and why what goes where when who is with who. You follow me? *(Actor isn't sure.)* All right. I'm going to talk slower. Cassidy is a dyke.

ACTOR: A dyke?

PUBLICIST: Not a big dyke. Not a hairy Amazon or anything. A lipstick dyke, if you will, very stylish, discreet with her tattoos. Nevertheless, butch as a bull. Now I have no problem with this, nor does anyone else I associate with. People have a right to be whatever they're stuck with, and I applaud that. But regrettably, the major viewing public is not so well-informed. When they see a love scene between a guy and a girl, and they know the girl is really a guy, it confuses them. They say, "Hey, why is she giving him the tongue? She doesn't really like men! This isn't real!"

ACTOR: Of course it isn't real. It's a *movie*. They're *acting*. Dustin Hoffman wasn't really autistic.

PUBLICIST: You and I know that. A lot of people out there don't. So it's in everyone's best interests to see that the pubic remains unconfused. This is where you come in.

ACTOR: Where?

PUBLICIST: I see a lot of Harrison Ford in you. You got the build for an action star, plus you got the sensitive thing going, perfect for chick flicks, those neo-Gothic Jane Austen wet dreams. Daniel Day Lewis, that's who I'm thinking of — fuck Harrison Ford. No, I'm telling you, you could be a major star for years to come. So any reason why you can't get married?

ACTOR: Married?

PUBLICIST: Any legal encumbrances, palimony suits, unfashionable addictions? Let me know now, because I warn you, Cassidy is one of those women who sets incredibly high standards for everyone but herself.

ACTOR: You're talking about me marrying Cassidy Velour?

PUBLICIST: Have we been discussing someone else? Did I just have an aneurysm or something? Yes, Cassidy Velour, America's Sweetheart. We at FailSafe happen to think it's a good match. What do you think?

ACTOR: I don't even know her.

PUBLICIST: What's to know? Look, she's already given us the go-ahead to approach you. She's seen some of your tapes, she likes your height and your coloring. You might have to change your name, though. She doesn't like "Jarrod." Too trendy.

ACTOR: But she *is* a lesbian?

PUBLICIST: That's the point, Einstein. You get married, stay together for three years, and then have an amicable divorce. Just long enough to establish her estrogen level. In the meantime your film career goes right to the express lane. FailSafe will guarantee you a starring role in at least five medium to big-budget films, with top names, top directors, top caterers. We'll invest in your future if you'll invest in our present. Did I say that right? *(Runs it through his head.)* Yeah. So what's your take on this, champ?

ACTOR: Well — it surprises me. I thought lesbianism was ultra-chic in Hollywood.

PUBLICIST: That was last week. We're all getting pretty tired of lesbians. You know what the new fad is now? Bestiality.

ACTOR: *(Sighs.)* So much is timing.

PUBLICIST: So shall we shake on it? Can we green-light this baby? *(Shakes Actor's hand.)* Now if you'll excuse me, I think I'm missing my pre-landing beverage.

(The Publicist heads back to his own seat.)

Actor!
Frederick Stroppel

Comic

Actor and Zed (both twenties to thirties)

> This play is a surreal, very funny satire about the actor's life, focusing on the story of one actor from birth through The End. Here, the actor is hanging out in a trendy Hollywood café, where he meets an old friend named Zed, who's a writer.

ACTOR: Cassidy can be a downer at times, but she means well. And she did get me the three million. *(Actor enters the Formica Café.)* But sometimes you just want to get away from all the bullshit about first-week grosses and contract points. You want to rediscover your love for the art of acting. That's when I head for the Formica Café, a dusty relic of Old Hollywood. The Formica is where all the industry types hang out to forget about the industry. *(Actor gets a drink, waves to various cronies and colleagues. He spots Zed at the bar.)* Hey, Zed.

ZED: Jarrod!

ACTOR: Campbell.

ZED: Right. How's it going? You're a big star now.

ACTOR: *(Shrugs.)* A moderate star at best. Three mil for my next picture. You're doing OK?

ZED: I'm writing for a sit-com. It's a cartoon, actually. Which has its advantages. No actors. *(Sighs.)* I have to get out of television.

ACTOR: Hear anything from Taylor?

ZED: Yeah, she's back in New York. She's doing a one-woman show on Theater Row.

ACTOR: The Martha Stewart thing?

ZED: No, Shakespeare.

ACTOR: Shakespeare!

ZED: Pretty clever. She took all these lines from the plays and sonnets and put together the life story of Anne Hathaway. It's called *That Strafford Girl.*

ACTOR: Why didn't I think of that angle? Well, I'm happy for her. Taylor's a sweet, lovely girl. She didn't belong in L.A. No teeth in her sphincter, you know?

ZED: I guess. Anyway, I've got something exciting in the works, a feature project based on my screenplay about the horrors of Tourette's Syndrome.

ACTOR: Tourette's Syndrome?

ZED: It's the story of a man and his struggle not to be heard. You would be fantastic in the part, now that I think of it.

ACTOR: Sounds like a challenge.

ZED: Want to take a look at it?

ACTOR: Sure, I'd love to. Send me a copy.

ZED: I have one right here.

(Zed pulls one out of his bag.)

ACTOR: *(Unenthused.)* Great. *(Hefts it.)* Oo. Heavy.

ZED: Are you going to read it?

ACTOR: Sure. When I have time. I'm so fucking busy.

ZED: You're not going to read it, are you?

ACTOR: Of course I'm going to read it. Jesus. When I have the time.

(Beat.)

ZED: You know, Campbell, we go way back — back when you were Bronson. I have to say, I've always admired your drive, your resilience. Your musculature.

(Zed rubs Actor's shoulder sensually, and he moves to his neck.)

ACTOR: What are you doing?

ZED: Could I confess something to you?

ACTOR: Could you possibly not?

ZED: I've always considered us good friends. But in my heart I've always hoped we could be more than that.

ACTOR: What?

ZED: I think you know I've always cared for you, deeply.

ACTOR: What are you saying? — Stop rubbing me — You're gay? Since when?

ZED: Since I came to terms with myself. Since I decided to stop living a lie . . . Since I want you to read the damn script, OK?

ACTOR: Look, Zed, it's a nice try, but I'm not interested.

ZED: You don't have to put on the macho act, I know you've always had a crush on me.

ACTOR: Are you joking? I mean, use your head: Even if I were gay, I wouldn't have a crush on a TV *writer.* And besides, I'm a married man.

ZED: Oh, everybody knows that's a setup.

ACTOR: Everybody knows . . . ?

ZED: Sure. You married Cassidy Velour to divert attention from your private life. We all know how that works . . .

ACTOR: Let me just tell you that you're 180 degrees off the mark here.

ZED: Really? Are you in love with her? Are you sleeping with her?

ACTOR: Contractually I can't comment on any of this.

ZED: All right, so — just a blow job. Please. It will make me happy, knowing that I did everything I could to get this project off the ground.

ACTOR: I'll read the screenplay, I promise.

ZED: Let me blow you anyway. For my own peace of mind.

ACTOR: No, really.

ZED: It's like a verbal handshake.

ACTOR: People are looking . . .

ZED: An oral contract.

ACTOR: You can pay for my drink.

ZED: *Please* let me blow you! I won't sleep tonight! *Please!*

ACTOR: *(Sighs.)* All right. But just once. And remember, this is a big favor. You owe me. *(Actor and Zed walk off. Offscreen; moaning.)* Ohh . . . Ohhhh . . . !

The General From America

Richard Nelson

Dramatic

Andre (late twenties) and Arnold (late thirties)

> This is a fine play that tries to separate myth from men in dealing
> with the story of the notorious Revolutionary War traitor Benedict
> Arnold. In this scene, Arnold, commander of the fort at West Point,
> makes his first contact with Major Andre, his go-between with the
> British high command.

> *Haverstraw, five miles south of West Point. A field overlooking the Hud-*
> *son River. Night.*

ANDRE: *(Offstage.)* Mr. Monk? Is that you? *(Andre, out of uniform, enters,*
holding up a lantern.) Sir?
(Arnold enters from the opposite direction. Short pause.)

ARNOLD: Mr. — Anderson?
(They look at each other for a moment. Andre hears something and turns
to where Arnold has entered.)

ANDRE: Who's that?

ARNOLD: My orderly. He'll keep his distance.

ANDRE: Wouldn't it be best to . . .

ARNOLD: *(Turns and calls.)* Sergeant, stay with the horses! *(Back to Andre.)*
Why aren't you in uniform?

ANDRE: *(Ignoring him, looking off.)* What a thrilling night. Is it not? One
could not imagine anything more dramatic.

ARNOLD: It's an area I'm very fond of — the Hudson.

ANDRE: I've journeyed up it myself. Soon after I arrived in this country.
To Quebec. To fight you, General. *(Arnold looks at him.)* I'm a great
fan of yours. You've been quite the thorn in the side. I admire that.
Soldier to soldier.

ARNOLD: *(Looks toward the Hudson.)* Your ship, the *Vulture* — it's staying too close. My men will shell it. It should move off and come back — for the pickup.

ANDRE: Perhaps we should go now then. While it's there. You've brought nothing with you? *(Beat.)* Or are you still unsure?

ARNOLD: *(Suddenly.)* How committed are you British to winning this war?

ANDRE: Sir, I can promise —

ARNOLD: *(Over this.)* Do you have the stomach for it? I have wondered that often enough. Your army sits in New York —

ANDRE: Sir Henry believes patience —

ARNOLD: I need to know the depth of your passion! I need to know if you *believe!* And that you will act justly and honorably upon your beliefs! *(Beat.)* Have I made myself clear?
(Beat.)

ANDRE: I can assure you, sir, that as long as there's an England, these colonies will be *of* that England. You have my word. Sir Henry Clinton is as committed to this cause as he is to his own life. And I, sir, am willing to suffer a painful death for its noble sake. *(Short pause. Arnold says nothing.)* Should we go? *(There is no response.)* We haven't talked compensation. *(Arnold turns to hear this.)* For such a brave act as this, my government expects to pay — something. Out of gratitude. Having you on our side will do much for morale, for one thing. What are you seeking?

ARNOLD: *(After some hesitation.)* I wish only to be given what I'm already owed by Congress, both in back pay and loans made. *(Beat.)* And — for the value of my property in New Haven, which shall surely be confiscated when my actions here become known.
(Arnold looks at Andre.)

ANDRE: Do you have a figure amount?

ARNOLD: In pounds?

ANDRE: What else is there?
(Beat.)

ARNOLD: Ten thousand. And this constitutes no profit on my behalf. Only reimbursement —

ANDRE: I understand —

ARNOLD: And pay for what I'm giving up. My claim's now in — I do not wish to end up indigent in my —

ANDRE: I understand. And what you ask seems fair —

ARNOLD: *(Over this.)* I am no Judas. This is not how I see myself, nor how I wish to be seen. I do not do this for money! It is my hope that my actions here will give courage to others to do the same. And if I accept no more than what I'm owed, then the virtue of what I do can't be questioned. It will be seen that I act in good conscience, honor intact, and for what is in the best interest of my country.
(Beat.)

ANDRE: I salute you. It is indeed a noble thing you do. I am in a position to guarantee the request. *(Andre looks at Arnold, expecting him to go with him now, but Arnold hesitates, then sits on the ground. Andre takes out a flask.)* Would you like a . . . ? *(He notices that the flask is nearly empty.)* I have another. *(He takes out another, offers it to Arnold, who ignores it. Then Andre takes a big swig himself. In fact, it slowly becomes clear that Andre is a bit drunk already. Andre, to be friendly, sits on the ground as well. After a pause.)* Beautiful night. How is your lovely wife? I assume she must be . . . ? She'll be joining you, I assume.

ARNOLD: She's fine. *(Beat. For a moment he is lost in thought.)* She says you're a — poet?

ANDRE: *(Smiling.)* I've written —

ARNOLD: *(Over this.)* And actor. She talks about a ball, when you were in Philadelphia.

ANDRE: *(Over this.)* The Meschianza.

ARNOLD: I can never understand what she's — it sounds so — it doesn't make sense.

ANDRE: *(Over the end of this.)* A little something to keep the men's spirits up. A festival really. To celebrate General Howe's return to London. *(Beat.)* I created a tilt and tournament, like those of the ancient knights. We had armor; I was in charge of the hats myself. I could step into the life of a milliner now. Should one want that. *(Beat.)* We had jousts. The ladies dressed in Turkish costume. Your wife was adorable. It was fun. Everyone in Philadelphia had fun. Everyone invited. It cost a fortune. *(He laughs.)* It was like a play, but without an audience, only actors. The Knights of the Blended Rose. Their motto: "We droop when separated." *(He laughs and drinks.)* The Knights of the Burning Mountain. Their motto: "I burn forever." *(He smiles.)* We redid a whole mansion. You walk in and it's like — hundreds of years ago. It got us through the winter. The General was very pleased.

(Beat.)

ARNOLD: My wife had a good time.

ANDRE: My greatest achievement in America — so far. It's why I'm a major. Caused a hell of a lot of resentment — my promotion. But this — *(Gestures toward Arnold.)* — will change everything for me. *(Beat.)* Sir, I think we should go.

ARNOLD: I am not coming with you today, Major Andre.

ANDRE: *(Suddenly standing and angry.)* Then what am I doing here? Why did you insist that I come? I do not enjoy wasting my time —

ARNOLD: I asked you to come — *(He gets Andre's attention.)* — so that I could offer you not only myself, but my command, the three forts at West Point, and its three thousand eighty-six men. They are yours. *(Andre is stunned. After a pause.)*

ANDRE: And how is such an offer — to be accepted? Will you march them down the river —

ARNOLD: *(Takes maps and papers out of his coat.)* A tally of my army's strength, maps of the forts, with locations of weakness marked. A copy of the plan in event of alarm, again with weaknesses indicated. A proposed attack plan, including strength needed, types of equipment and so forth. You will see that, as presently organized, West Point stands completely vulnerable, to even the most modest assault. And with myself in charge of the defenders, there can be no chance of failure. *(He holds out maps and papers to Andre.)* Is it now clear why I insisted that we meet?

ANDRE: *(Walking around, excited.)* My God, they'll make me a bloody general. And they laugh at me now. I know they do. *(To Arnold.)* I came to this godforsaken country because — I was a bloody clerk at home. They wouldn't even let me become an actor! So I'm here. Three thousand men! *(He opens the flask. Offering.)* Please . . .

ARNOLD: I'm not finished. *(Beat.)* This assault must be taken tomorrow night. For good reason. This morning, in a few hours, a guest will arrive in my house. I shall spend the day with him, showing him the weakness of our fortifications. This will disappoint him, but not make him suspicious. Because he visits in part to make amends for errors made toward me. *(Beat.)* I will forgive him. Embrace him. And he will spend the night. *(Beat.)* He is General George Washington. Commander in chief of our army. With the capture of West Point, you capture him. *(Beat.)* A good man. He's supported me throughout my political troubles, coming to my aid again and again. There have been times when I saw him as my father. *(Short pause.)* You achieve this, Major, and the war is over. *(Silence. The wind. Then birds are heard overhead. Arnold looks up.)* They should be asleep.

(Cannon fire is heard offstage.)

ANDRE: What's that?

ARNOLD: My men are firing on your ship. You'd better signal to be picked up. I dare not order them to stop *(More cannon fire. Andre takes a swig from his flask. Arnold watches where the cannon shot hits the river.)* They're close. Your ship can't send a launch now.

ANDRE: What am I going — ?

ARNOLD: *(Over this.)* I'll get a couple of men from the battery to row you over. I'll tell them — you're taking messages from me. *(Andre takes another swig.)* Just signal for them not to leave!

ANDRE: General. You are the first true American patriot.

ARNOLD: Don't kiss my ass, Major. I've never found that pleasant. And do stop drinking. *(Arnold looks at Andre.)* My God, have I made a mistake?

ANDRE: You haven't, sir. I give you my word. And I am sober. *(He takes the flask and throws it into the woods.)* Good day, sir. And good fortune.

Paradise
Chris Edmond

Dramatic

Clive (thirty); Scott (thirty)

> Clive is visiting California from London to direct a play. A colleague,
> Scott, a highly self-destructive man, who is sharing a house with Clive,
> confronts him in a drunken stupor.

*Scott is extremely drunk and holding a beer. Clive enters. Scott leaps out
at him.*

SCOTT: *(As Jack Nicholson in* The Shining.*)* Here's Johnny!

CLIVE: Jesus, Scott!

SCOTT: This is Buckhorn beer. Very masculine name don't you think?

CLIVE: Butch as Kong.

SCOTT: Hey, I was looking at some photos of your wife.

CLIVE: She's not actually my . . . Look, those photos were in my suitcase.

SCOTT: Look man, it was unlocked.

CLIVE: Look *man,* I lost the key . . . anyway . . .

SCOTT: She's pretty.

CLIVE: Yes.

SCOTT: You must trust her.

CLIVE: Yes.

SCOTT: That's very foolish.

CLIVE: What?

SCOTT: Fool-ish.

CLIVE: I don't think so.

SCOTT: No?

CLIVE: Going through my stuff is a bit, well, fucking abnormal.

SCOTT: Loved the pink toothbrush Clive.

CLIVE: It goes with the eyes. I'm glad you like my room . . . when are you
moving in?

SCOTT: Is that an offer?

CLIVE: No.

> *(Pause.)*

CLIVE: What's that smell?

SCOTT: My aftershave.

CLIVE: It reminds me of something.

> *(Scott pours beer over his shirt.)*

CLIVE: Good God.

SCOTT: This beer is American piss. Don't drink it. You should try LaBatt Blue. Canadian. This shirt is from Canada. Plaid.

CLIVE: Very fetching.

SCOTT: I wash it regularly that's why it's so faded. Nice blue though isn't it? Like the sky, or any eternity. *(Pause.)* I'd better get to bed. I feel tired and I need a sleep. Help yourself to beer, American piss or not . . . oh and Nye thinks you drink too much.

CLIVE: Oh.

SCOTT: Read through my lesson plans if you want. I'll leave them for you.

CLIVE: I'm only here for a couple of months.

SCOTT: Or so. Another time then.

CLIVE: You want me to call you in the morning?

SCOTT: No. *(Pause.)* Good night. *(Attempts to kiss Clive. Pause. Scott quotes Brecht with drunken dignity:)* "But they call up the strength to sweat up the stony paths with their baskets, to bear children, yes even to eat, from the feeling of continuity and necessity which is given them by the sight of the soil, of the trees springing with the new green foliage every year, of the little church and by listening every Sunday to the Bible texts."

CLIVE: Beautiful. *(Pause.)* What is it?

SCOTT: *(He laughs.)* Just acting.

CLIVE: Just.

> *(Pause.)*

SCOTT: You want to come?

CLIVE: What?

SCOTT: To bed. *(Pause.)* For a fuck. *(Pause.)*

CLIVE: No Scott

SCOTT: Fuck you then. *Fuck you.*

> *(Lights fade.)*

Speaking in Tongues
Andrew Bovell

Dramatic

Leon and Pete (both thirties to forties)

> This scene takes place in a bar. Pete has just left his wife because he found out she was having an affair. Little does he know that the guy he's talking to is his wife's lover.

> *A bar. Leon is drinking alone. Pete enters. He looks agitated. He feels a sharp pain in his chest. Leon looks over.*

LEON: Are you all right?

PETE: Yeah.

LEON: Are you sure?

PETE: Yeah. *(He breathes through the pain.)* I just get this pain in my chest . . . sometimes.

LEON: Your heart?

PETE: I'm not sure. Could just be indigestion. Or an ulcer.

LEON: Or a mild heart attack.

PETE: Well, could be, yeah.

LEON: You see I get a pain like that too sometimes.

PETE: Yeah? Have you had it checked out.

LEON: No. You?

PETE: No. *(Beat.)* I've just had this really bad experience.

LEON: What?

PETE: Just before. Just a moment ago.

LEON: What happened?

PETE: I don't know what happened. I was walking along the street, just thinking a few things through, certainly minding my own business, and I passed this woman and she started screaming at me.

LEON: What for?

PETE: Christ, I don't know. She thought I said something to her or something. She started screaming at me, saying I accosted her. Calling for witnesses. Threatening to press charges. It was just awful.

LEON: Was she mad or something?

PETE: She didn't look mad. She was well dressed. Quite, you know, well-to-do, and she just started screaming at me. And everybody was looking at me as though I had done something wrong. You know, suddenly I was this villain. And somebody ran off to get the cops and I thought shit how did I get caught up in this so I started to run which just made it look like I was a total arsehole who had tried to hurt this woman or something but I swear I didn't do anything to her.

LEON: It's all right.

PETE: Jesus, I didn't touch her.

LEON: It's all right. You didn't touch her. Just relax. You're going to cause yourself another attack.

PETE: Nothing like that's ever happened to me before.

LEON: It's OK.

PETE: I don't look for trouble.

LEON: It's finished.

PETE: Yeah . . . I know. I'm all right now. Shit. I'm sorry. I didn't mean to just come out with all that. I'm sorry.

LEON: You all right now?

PETE: Yeah it's gone now.

LEON: Are you sure?

PETE: Yeah, honestly.

LEON: Well . . . if you need help . . .

PETE: Thanks. But I'm fine. Go back to your drink, please.

LEON: I'm sorry. I'll leave you.

PETE: Are you a Good Samaritan or something?

LEON: No. No. Definitely not. I just thought you might be in trouble.

PETE: Thanks, but I'm fine.

LEON: I mean, Jesus, do I look like a Good Samaritan or something?

PETE: No.

LEON: No. There you go.

PETE: You look like a cop.

LEON: A what?

PETE: A cop.

LEON: Really?

PETE: Are you?

LEON: Well, yeah I am, but I never thought I looked like one.

PETE: It was just a guess.

LEON: What is it? The haircut or something?

PETE: No, it was just a feeling.

LEON: I feel like a cop?

PETE: Well, I don't know, yeah you do.

LEON: Shit.

PETE: It's weird.

LEON: What is?

PETE: I've never had a conversation with a cop before. I mean outside of them being a policeman. You know what I mean.

LEON: What? You've never spoken with a policeman before?

PETE: Yeah, plenty of times.

LEON: Plenty of times?

PETE: Well . . .

LEON: What for?

PETE: Well, you know, on police business. Traffic fines or once my house was broken into. And once my wife was caught . . . *(He hesitates.)*

LEON: What?

PETE: I shouldn't really tell you, I guess.

LEON: Shoplifting?

PETE: Yes, how did you know?

LEON: Just a guess.

PETE: Really?

LEON: Don't be embarrassed.

PETE: I'm not. Well actually I am. I mean, I was at the time. I mean, how would you feel if your wife was a shoplifter?

LEON: I'd feel pretty bad.

PETE: Exactly.

LEON: So, is she still doing it?

PETE: What? No. Absolutely not. It was a one-of thing. A mistake.

LEON: Sure.

PETE: She made a mistake and she was caught.

LEON: It happens.

PETE: End of story.

LEON: Fine . . . I'm sorry but you've got me worried now. How did you know I was a cop?

PETE: I told you. It was just a feeling. I didn't think I'd be right.

LEON: It's not the haircut?

PETE: No. Plenty of people have haircuts like that. *(Beat.)*

LEON: Are you waiting for someone or something?

PETE: No. I just thought I'd have a drink.

LEON: Ah. *(Pause.)*

PETE: I don't usually drink by myself.

LEON: I've been known to.

PETE: Trouble at home. Taking refuge. You know how it is.

LEON: Yeah.

PETE: Are you married?

LEON: Just.

PETE: Well . . . then you understand.

LEON: I don't understand anything about marriage.

PETE: Nor do I. Haven't a clue. *(Beat.)* Truth is I come home the other night and I go to kiss my wife, oh shit, sorry. Why am I telling you this?

LEON: It's all right.

PETE: No. No. Listen . . . *(I'm sorry.)*

LEON: It's kind of easier to tell these things to a stranger. *(Pete shrugs.)* There's nothing at stake. You tell me what you want to tell me. I tell you what I want to tell you. We both go away a little wiser. No loss. No shame.

PETE: I've left my wife.

LEON: Ah . . . well, there you go, my wife's left me.

PETE: Permanent?

LEON: I don't know. I hope not.

PETE: Do you still love her?

LEON: Oh yeah, I love her. I hurt her though, very badly. And she's gone away. Maybe to punish me. Maybe to recover. I don't know and I've just got to wait. But I've never been very good at it.

PETE: At what?

LEON: Waiting . . . And you? Do you love your wife?

PETE: I can't tell you. Because I don't know. I'm finding it hard to forgive.

LEON: What do you have to forgive her for?

PETE: She . . .

LEON: What?

PETE: You know.

LEON: Had an affair?

PETE: Yeah. That. Well, just kind of a one-night thing. I mean, I think. I hope that's all it is.

LEON: Yeah, I'm sure that's all it is.

PETE: You?

LEON: Same. Except the other way around.

PETE: Huh?

LEON: I had the affair. Or the one-night thing.

PETE: You bastard.

LEON: Yeah.

PETE: Funny thing is I nearly had one too. That's what really pisses me off.

LEON: That she did and you didn't.

PETE: That I came this close *(Holding up two fingers to indicate a tiny length.)* and pulled back because, in the end, I thought I had a reason to. But Jane obviously didn't.

LEON: Who?

PETE: Jane. That's my wife. That's why I can't forgive. *(Leon gets a pain in his chest.)* Are you OK?

LEON: Yeah . . . I just need a minute.

PETE: You sure . . . should I get help?

LEON: No . . . it's fine. It's going. *(Leon waits for the pain to subside.)*

PETE: You right?

LEON: Yep. Fine. It's gone. Just came and went.

PETE: You should go and see someone.

LEON: Yeah. So should you. *(Beat.)* You know your wife, Jane, you know this thing, with the other guy, it probably didn't mean much.

PETE: That's not the point.

LEON: You've got to be able to forgive. These things, in the scheme of things, in a marriage, in a lifetime, they don't mean much.

PETE: Well, maybe not to you.

LEON: People make mistakes.

PETE: Maybe.

LEON: Yeah, they do. People fuck up. In a marriage you've got to see people through those fuckups.

PETE: But you have to say that.

LEON: Do I?

PETE: Yeah, you're in the same position as Jane. You did something really dirty to your wife. You treated her badly. That's not just a fuckup. That's something fundamental. That's betrayal. And now you want forgiveness for that. But if I forgive you . . .

LEON: You forgive me?

PETE: I mean if your wife forgives you, or I forgive Jane, then that's an invitation to do it all over again.

LEON: No.

PETE: That's like saying, hey, I understand, you're human, you're fallible . . .

LEON: You're really black-and-white about things, aren't you?

PETE: About this I am, yeah. You're human, you're fallible. You've made a mistake. But that's not a mistake. At least not an honest one. That's a calculated betrayal. And that's one of the cruelest things you can do to someone.

LEON: But you would have got it out of your system.

PETE: That's bullshit. That's utter bullshit. It's just the opposite. You've had a taste and it was easy and you might think you won't do it again but next year, next month, hell, next week the same things will come up between you and your wife and you'll say it worked then, why not again. But this time it won't be just once. You'll sleep with the woman more than once. And then, well, it's a whole other situation because then there are expectations. You've gone into something and you won't get out of it without someone being hurt. That's why I left. Because there're repercussions and to forgive is to say those repercussions don't matter. But they do matter. To me they matter.

LEON: Yeah . . . but do you love your wife?

PETE: I told you. I don't know.

LEON: No. Love's not like that. If you love someone, you know it. If you don't, you know it. I mean a lot of people kid themselves. A lot of people let love slip into habit. But the truth's the truth and everybody knows theirs. So do you love your wife?

PETE: Yeah . . . I love her.

LEON: Then let me tell you this. Forgive her. And if you can't, then get even. Get back on an equal par. Go out, tonight, tomorrow night, some night, find someone, sleep with them, feel the comfort of their body, have some fun. Whatever. But get rid of your "I've been hard done by" kind of attitude and go back to Jane and get on with your life. *(They are silent for a moment.)*

PETE: My name's Pete . . . by the way.

LEON: Nice to meet you, Pete.

PETE: Yours?

LEON: Ah . . . Harold.

PETE: Harold? You don't look like a Harold.

Take Me Out
Richard Greenberg

Dramatic

Davey (mid to late thirties); Darren (mid to late twenties)

> During the height of a pennant race Darren Lemming, the biggest
> star on a team not unlike the Yankees, has decided to reveal to his
> teammates, to the press, and to the fans that he is gay. Needless to
> say, this opens up a hornet's nest of controversy. Here, Darren vio-
> lates baseball etiquette by going into the opposing team's clubhouse
> to talk things over with his friend and mentor, an older player on
> another team named Davey. Darren is confused, and needs Davey's
> sage counsel; but Davey is appalled by what Darren has done and,
> truth be told, by what has been revealed.

DARREN: I . . . uh . . . we haven't talked . . .

DAVEY: No, Darren, we haven't . . .

DARREN: . . . You get my messages, Davey?

DAVEY: Now, that's very interesting, Darren. That's a very interesting way
to *put it.* Did I get your messages? Not your "message," not singu-
lar — no, you ask: Did I get your messages? And I can only answer:
some of them. Some I *failed* to get. Some, it seems, were never *sent.*

DARREN: Shit, Davey, it was just a *ques*tion —

DAVEY: Don't touch me!

DARREN: I'm ten feet away from ya, Davey —

DAVEY: And we should keep that distance. We should maintain that distance from which things can be seen in their *entirety.*

DARREN: . . . OK.

DAVEY: This is a day of *reck*oning.

(Darren makes a lightly scoffing sound.)

DAVEY: Are you *fleering* at me, Darren?

DARREN: I wouldn't know it if I was. Fleering! Why do you talk like you
were born a hundred years ago?

DAVEY: And what if I do?

DARREN: I dunno.

It's just a little uncontemporary.

DAVEY: And is that a *bad* thing, Darren? Do we *value* the present over all other epochs? Do we think everything has evolved in the direction of the good? Or has some of it — most of it — been a sliding back. A devolution?

DARREN: Aw, shit, you're not gonna start disclaimin' dinosaurs on me and stuff, are ya?

DAVEY: I'm just saying, Darren, that it is more often than not a *small* mind that considers itself en*light*ened. That en*light*enment is most often an inability to see the darkness that surrounds you. *(Beat.)*

DARREN: This isn't gonna go well, is it?

DAVEY: Oh, I think it is. I think it is going to go well, Darren. How can things go badly when two people speak their truth? *(Beat.)*

DARREN: Fleer.

DAVEY: *Are you making mock of me?*

DARREN: Only a little, Davey — the way you like —

DAVEY: That's over.

DARREN: . . . OK.

DAVEY: Who the *fuck* are you, man? What the *fuck* do you think you're doing here?

DARREN: I —

DAVEY: What kind of *mess* do you find it fit to make? What kind of *nonsense* are you putting out in the world?

DARREN: I —

DAVEY: *"I!" "I!"* Stop saying "I" — you don't know the meaning of the word —

DARREN: But I do, Davey —

DAVEY: *Shit,* man, we all have *demons.* Some of us less disgusting ones than yours — but we shut up about them! Take them into little rooms, *wrestle* with them there — present a good face to the world — till our demons are slain and we *become* what we claim we *are.* What kind of sordidness is this you've got going on? Why did you feel the *need* to splash your ugliness all over everything?

DARREN: You told me to.

DAVEY: . . . Oh, so now you feel some need to add *slander* to the mischief?

DARREN: I thought you were givin' me a sorta per*mis*sion, Davey, I thought you were bein' . . . *kind.*

DAVEY: You twist everything.

DARREN: You told me to reveal my true nature. You said I could only do this through love.

DAVEY: That's before I knew you were a pervert. *(Beat.)*

DARREN: Oh. *(Beat.)* You said you knew me to be good. I . . . loved you very much for that, Davey —

DAVEY: Have you just been wanting to *fuck* me for eight years, Darren?

DARREN: No.

DAVEY: Have I been your *beard?*

DARREN: My . . . ?

DAVEY: Oh, everybody knows Davey Battle's good, Davey Battle's a religious man, a continent man — nobody going around with Davey Battle's going to be whoring, nobody going around with Davey Battle's going to be chasing tail — was that the whole thing, Darren?

DARREN: I don't — think so —

DAVEY: Then *what?*

DARREN: I liked you. *(Beat.)*

DAVEY: You lie.

DARREN: Fuck you —

DAVEY: You lie in your heart —

DARREN: Fuck you, Davey, fuck you —

DAVEY: And until you correct yourself —

DARREN: *Fuck* yourself, man — *fuck* yourself —

DAVEY: You will welter in profanity and vulgarity and every kind of ugliness.

DARREN: You're right. Yes, you're right. I need to clean up my language I need to make my language family-appropriate while, at the same time, conveyin' the *truth* of my heart, so let me just put it *this* way, Davey: Drop dead.

Take Me Out
Richard Greenberg

Seriocomic

Darren (mid to late twenties); Mason (late thirties to midforties)

This is the final scene in this wonderful play about what might happen if a major sports superstar came out of the closet to reveal that he is gay. Darren is that superstar, and Mason is the nebbish-y, borderline middle-aged gay man who handles his money. Mason has become an unabashed baseball fan. This scene takes place on the baseball field, at the end of the last game of the season.

MASON: *(Singing.)* "Oh my man, I love him so, he'll never know . . . *(He giggles.)*

DARREN: Are you drunk?

MASON: I *had* a beer.

DARREN: You had a keg.

MASON: No. Just one. The great advantage of an extremely narrow life is the slightest deviation produces *stag*gering results. *(He giggles.)* Oh, I'm sorry if I'm silly.

DARREN: No, it's kinda cute. Kinda endearing . . .

MASON: Oh . . . well . . . yes, it is . . .

DARREN: . . . So, Mason, I was wonderin' . . .

MASON: Yes?

DARREN: If I retire now, will I —

MASON: Oh no no no no no *no* — not the night you won the World *Series!* My God, man, have you no sense of oc*ca*sion?

DARREN: I just need to be alone for a while. I just need to get real quiet. I'm not who I was when the season started.

MASON: Neither am I — isn't it *great?*

DARREN: But ya see, unlike you, I *liked* who I . . . But I guess I really wasn't that then, either.

MASON: . . . Darren, I truly, deeply feel I should be responding to your *crise* right now, but all I keep thinking is, when do you get the *ring?*

DARREN: The —

MASON: The championship —

DARREN: Oh, next year.

MASON: Well, then you *have* to come back, you don't have a choice —

DARREN: *(Flashing rings.)* I already have two others.

MASON: Oh! Is *that* what those are?

DARREN: What didja think?

MASON: I didn't know. I just thought you had terrible taste! Wow! Look at them.

DARREN: Yeah —

MASON: Well, all you have to do is look at them, and you'll know.

DARREN: Know what?

MASON: Who you are. Your ontological quandary will be disspelled.

DARREN: They just mean I was on a winning team, that's all.

MASON: That's a better start than most of us get. Don't diminish it, it would be too ungrateful.

DARREN: *(Still sad.)* I s'pose. *(Beat.)* I guess I have to go to this *party. (Beat.)* Do you wanna come?

MASON: Huh?

DARREN: Wanna be my date?

MASON: Don't you have a date?

DARREN: No.

MASON: How can you not have a date?

DARREN: I told you — I don't know people.

MASON: But you didn't mean that.

DARREN: But I did. *(Beat.)* Come on. We'll get photographed together, splashed over alla tabloids. Everybody'll think you're my long-awaited *boy*friend. Those two gay guys down the hall will drop dead. *(A hitch as he hears this, brief, then:)* Then I won't hafta kiss you in the elevator like we've both been dreading.

MASON: . . . OK. Um. Yes! But do I look . . . all right?

DARREN: You look OK . . . You could maybe use an accessory —

MASON: I don't — have —

DARREN: *(Pulling off one of his rings.)* Hey — wear this.

MASON: What?

DARREN: Yeah — it'll be a goof — come on. *(He slips the ring on Mason's finger.)* That feels weird, doesn't it?

MASON: Wow.

(Mason spreads his fingers in front of him to inspect the ring.)

DARREN: Hey, Mars — it's gonna be a roomful of *jocks.*

(He folds his fingers into a fist, demonstrates looking at the ring that way.)

MASON: Oh . . . oh.

DARREN: So — whaddya say?

MASON: Sure. *(He starts to leave with Darren, pauses.)* Um — would it be all right if I met you there? If I stayed here just a little bit longer?

DARREN: You know where the place is?

MASON: I do, in fact.

DARREN: Sure. Enjoy yourself.

MASON: Thank you.

DARREN: Hey — Mars?

(Mason turns to Darren. Darren tosses him the ball. Mason catches it, gasps.)

DARREN: What a fuck of a season, huh?

MASON: Yes. It was. A fuck of a season. It was . . . tragic.

(Darren exits. To himself, realizing it.)

It *was* — tragic. *(A moment. His glance falls on the ring. Then moves to the ball. Then he closes his eyes and takes a deep breath, and opens his eyes, and takes in the whole stadium.)* What will we do till spring? *(Fade out.)*